HOVERMARINE

Published by Hellgate Press
(An imprint of L&R Publishing, LLC)

Hellgate Press
PO Box 3531
Ashland, OR 97520
email: sales@hellgatepress.com

Cover & Interior Design: L. Redding
ISBN: 978-1-954163-19-5

Printed and bound in the United States of America
First edition 10 9 8 7 6 5 4 3 2 1

HOVERMARINE

The Rise and Fall of a Pioneer in the High Speed Marine Market

William A. Zebedee • Michael R. Richards • Eaon W. Furnell
Roderick R. C. Wilkins • Graham A. Gifford • Peter White

HELLGATE PRESS ASHLAND, OREGON

HOVERMARINE

CONTENTS

BOOK ONE

BOOK TWO

(By Peter White)

INTRODUCING THE AUTHORS

This book is a joint effort by the authors, along with numerous other contributors who have reason to look back on their days with Hovermarine with a sense of pride; indeed a sense of belonging to something that was special. Even forty-plus years after the events we record here, we are still members of a fraternity that, for a period of our lives was the best of times.

We choose to start not with history or facts, but rather individual statements about what the Hovermarine story meant to us.

William A. Zebedee
Medford, Oregon, USA

What was so special about Hovermarine? In the end, the company failed and the technology did not survive, but for a moment in time, we soared.

When I invested in the company in 1970, the furthest thing from my mind was doing anything more than being an investor. However, the ink from my signature on the share-purchase check was barely dried when the company careened into its first disaster. Somebody had to do something! As I took a more active role, I started to realize that its employees were there for much more than a paycheck. They *believed* and they were survivors, in it for the long pull. Few people are afforded the privilege to lead such an organization.

In 1976 I uprooted my family from their comfortable existence in Pittsburgh, Pennsylvania and we moved to England. Why? Because I realized that I was not doing a proper job from a distance of 3,000 miles; because the people of Hovermarine deserved better from their leader.

And I loved being there! I couldn't wait to get in each morning, usually arriving by 5:00 a.m. My first stop typically was the shop floor to spend a few minutes with the night shift. Their dedication was palpable. They gave me the enthusiasm that would propel my day. This is very much their story.

Michael R. Richards
Chilbolton, Hants, UK

Having joined Hovermarine in the spring of 1973 as Financial Director, a year later I took over as Managing Director. There followed the most exciting, challenging, entertaining (and sometimes frustrating) seven years of my business career.

Hovermarine was a small company, with limited resources, but we did work with the most talented, willing, dedicated, hard-working but also fun loving group of people.

Everybody was on first name terms; there was no hierarchy or trade unions; there were no allocated parking spaces and no tiered expense allowances. Instead everybody had a common goal—to make a go of this fledgling business. And by any measure we achieved this.

This happened more than forty years ago, so inevitably my memories are pretty much of the highs, the lows, but mostly the people.

The highs include deals in Nigeria, France, Uruguay, Bolivia, some of which were absolutely critical to the survival of the company. (These were typically followed by general celebrations!) We secured Government funding for manufacturing, and for the HM 5 programme. The acquisition of Solaris gave us a badly needed work force and a huge manufacturing space.

The lows, which frankly were not so rare, included an almost constant liquidity battle, extensive travel—thirty-six hours to get to Montevideo via London, Paris, Rio, Buenos Aires; twenty-four hours to go from La Paz to Caracas; and the seven intolerable trips to Lagos speak for themselves. It was not always plain sailing, and in the slack periods sometimes we had to release personnel—this was by some measure the most unpleasant of all my responsibilities.

There were also some scrapes, including piracy (alleged) in France, arrest (threatened) in Montevideo, personal guarantees to fund wages, and the wife of the Korean ambassador falling into the river Itchen!

But it is the people I remember most; it's almost impossible to describe the camaraderie. Eaon Furnell (Manufacturing Director) and I used to play for the company football team (when selected—there was no favouritism). If we made a mistake, we were subjected to terrible abuse, and daren't show our faces on the shop floor the following day!

So it was a very sad day for me when in early 1980, I was invited by Sir John Rix to resign. In retrospect, this was a relief, because there was no way I could ever have fitted into the Vosper ethos and culture. The parting was without rancor.

Eaon W. Furnell
Wickham Fareham, Hants, UK

I was lucky to be invited to join the original Hovermarine Ltd in its early days back in 1966 as production engineer. I had been working at Southampton University in structural engineering, and was asked to test components of the hull of the then newly invented sidewall hovercraft.

Luck was not on our side and the company fell into receivership a few short years later. Fortunately, the company was reborn under its new American ownership and renamed Hovermarine Transport Ltd. These would be the very best years, when the company experienced dizzying growth and great friendships were formed that would last a lifetime. I loved it with all of the ups, downs and in betweens. Along the way, I was named production director.

I well remember thinking this company was truly different when our luck was down and I had to make men redundant. I always made a point of telling every individual myself. The majority always asked me to let them know when things picked up they could come back. Several went and came back more than once. This alone tells you we had something special.

In late 1983 I was appointed Managing Director. By then the Company was in a downward spiral which would prove unstoppable. Three years later I had the sad and difficult job of helping to sell the remnants of what had once been a great enterprise.

The actual beating heart of the company always resided in the employees in Woolston. The pressure and enthusiasm; the will to win amongst the staff and factory workers was real.

Roderick R.C. Wilkins
Dallas, Texas, USA

I joined Hovermarine in the late summer of 1976. I was a young lawyer (Solicitor), working in the City.

Hovermarine was looking for an in-house lawyer. After an initial introductory phone call, I was invited to an interview. I drove down to Woolston and met Bill Zebedee and Mike Richards. Bill is given to rapid decisions and so a month or so later I reported for work with the title Company Secretary.

Hovermarine was flooded with new orders. I was set to work with these and—at the same time became acquainted with the other side of the coin, the Company's portfolio of legal disputes and lawsuits. They ranged from major to minor—I believe there were more than fifteen—and in a dozen different countries. The following year we would purchase the assets of Solaris, but that came along with the yacht builder's recent bankruptcy and several half completed contracts.

What a wonderful set of opportunities! For my first few months I commuted daily from London to Southampton, but I was still motivated enough to get to work before 0800 most days. I learned the leadership group were all early starters. Bill Zebedee seemed to be always there first, standing tall, pacing the room and smoking an early cigar. Mike Richards, the MD, and Eaon Furnell were close behind him. The senior people had a sense of purpose and commitment. This had become obvious to the entire workforce and made the firm an unusual place to work in late 1970s England.

There was solidarity that was lacking in most of the rest of the country. Remember, this was a time of severe industrial and social unrest; garbage, coal and steel strikes and weekly "brownouts." The sense of overall purpose was very appealing.

A major feature of this was the lack of hierarchy. We all understood that Bill was our leader. As much as anything it was his talent and energy that made him that. However, the group of directors was strong willed—more a band of brothers than followers. The net result was that the board and senior managers were greater than the sum of their individual parts.

Graham A. Gifford
Maidenhead, Berkshire, UK

Back in the days when all young men in UK had to undergo two years' National Service, I joined the Royal Air Force. Nine years later, having spent most of this time as a Flight Lieutenant Navigator on Canberras (twin-engine fighter-bombers), I left the RAF for civvy street.

Firstly, I dabbled in early computers, but it soon became apparent that this was not my forte, so I applied to join British Hovercraft Corporation (BHC). BHC had made the world's first hovercraft and had a production line of larger hovercraft. All these craft were based on aircraft technology (lightweight aluminum structures and gas turbine engines) and sold into a marine environment. This resulted in uncompetitive prices, and I found the company's infrastructure and the means of conducting business archaic. So when I heard that Hovermarine Transport Ltd were looking for a Far East Sales Manager, I applied.

When I arrived at HTL, I liked the whole atmosphere of this small company far better than that of a large conglomerate such as BHC, and encouragingly there were direct and harmonious relationships between all the various departments. I soon settled down and started to make sales and, to capitalize on these sales, my family and I were moved out to The Philippines in 1976 and on to Singapore in 1978.

We came home from the Far East in 1980 when Vosper took over HTL, and I was then made responsible for worldwide sales under a new Sales Director. In fact, an abiding memory of my thirteen years employment with Hovermarine is a constant change of Sales Directors. As the old joke goes, "I said to my secretary, if my boss phones, take a note of his name." I remember nine bosses but I was happiest when reporting directly to Bill Zebedee during my period abroad—it was the only time I actually felt on the same wavelength as my boss!

I was made redundant in 1986, having just secured a sale of two HM221s for operation on the River Danube.

Peter White
Poway, California, USA

What other calling in the whole world could provide such diversity as running through the Sunda Straits between Java and Sumatra, under the shadow of the world renowned volcano Krakatoa, or skimming across the world's highest navigable lake to the sacred Inca Island of the Sun, or forging through dense tropical West African rainforests, or skirting the foreboding sand dunes on the edge of the Arabian Desert, where they meet the turbid waters of the Persian Gulf?

These and many more besides were amongst the daily thrills experienced whilst working with Hovermarine, the world's most significant builder of sidewall hovercraft.

Just eighteen days after being hired, and with a newly issued HM2 maintenance license in my pocket, I found myself outward bound on a seventeen-hour flight to the Philippines. Little did I know at that time that I was about to spend almost nine out of the next ten years outside of the UK.

BOOK ONE

Readers who are not familiar with the Hovermarine story may have noticed from the introductions of the authors that, for a number of years, four of the six authors constituted the top of the Company organization. Inevitably, our recounting of history has that perspective – the "Boardroom" for lack of a better term. However, prior to 1980, we were never a top-down organization.

With a total employment nearing 1,000 in 1979 and an operating reach that spanned thirty-six countries, we had relied on a team to build this enterprise. Book Two of this manuscript recounts the experiences of some of those team members who worked on the front lines.

Let's start with Book One, our view from the Boardroom....

HOVERMARINE

PART ONE

1966 – 1972

The Formative Years

HOVERMARINE

CHAPTER ONE

EARLY YEARS

IN 1965 TED TATTERSALL and a small group of associates formed Hovermarine Ltd. Their purpose was to produce high speed passenger ferries utilizing the technology known as side-wall hovercraft. The prototype structure was fabricated at Halmatic at its factory near Portsmouth and then fitted out at Camper & Nicholson Yachts on the River Itchen, near a property called Hazel Wharf, where Hovermarine was building a 35,000 sq.ft. factory and separate office block. Construction funding was being provided by the London Merchant Bankers, Baring Brothers, pursuant to a long term lease agreement.

The new facility was completed in 1967 and construction was begun on a series of seven craft, designated HM2.

The prototype, along with two more craft, was purchased in 1968 by British Rail Hovercraft for trial ferry services on various routes on the Solent in the South of England, the body of water separating Southampton from the Isle of Wight. Over the following year, four additional craft were completed and sold or leased to other British operators.

Early on, Hovermarine attracted the support of the National Research Development Council, a Crown Corporation whose charter was to safeguard and support British technology. A subsidiary, Hovercraft Development Ltd., held a broad portfolio of

The Woolston Works, Hovercraft World. July/August 1969

patents. In 1967, HDL granted Hovermarine a license plus some seed money to commercialize the concept.*

Even with HDL's support and early sales success, HM2s conversion from concept to reality was hardly encouraging. The original craft were plagued by mechanical issues and seaworthiness shortcomings, of which the latter would prove to be far more vexing. Once the HM2 achieved a speed sufficient to outrun its displacement, its structure (save the narrow catamaran-like sidewalls) was about thirty inches above water, theoretically allowing waves of less than thirty inches to pass under the hull. The problem was,

* Refer to Appendix B for a description of the relevant UK government agencies and their assistance to Hovermarine.

From drawing board to reality. HM2-003 on trials prior to delivery to the Bahamas.

of course, that Mother Nature doesn't produce uniform waves. Any higher rogue wave slammed into the bow of the hull, not only creating a very unpleasant ride, but slowing the craft sufficiently to bring it back down to its displacement mode.

With a management short on business experience and overwhelmed by technical issues, Hovermarine was forced into liquidation in early 1969. Its assets were then purchased by an American company called Transportation Technology Inc.

HOVERMARINE

CHAPTER TWO

ENTER TTI

TTI WAS INCORPORATED IN 1969 by a group of financial speculators from Dallas, Texas, expressly for the purpose of acquiring Hovermarine's assets from the liquidator. Knowing nothing about hovercraft, TTI's founders also hired four engineers who were researching surface effect technology at General Dynamics, a large U.S. defense contractor. The group had been given some small contracts by Defense Advanced Research Projects Agency (DARPA) to support their research.

TTI was looking for money to finance the operations. They sold the idea to the venture capital arm of A.G. Becker Inc., a Chicago brokerage house. Becker invited Bill Zebedee's small investment fund, based in Pittsburgh, Pennsylvania, to participate. Together they invested $500,000 in TTI. Zebedee was designated by the two investors to serve on TTI's board.

Bill continues: "Shortly thereafter, I attended my first meeting at the TTI offices in Dallas, Texas. Meeting most of the board members for the first time, I could see that I was dealing with a group of stereotypical Texas wheeler-dealers. Several were wearing neon suits that looked as if they would glow in the dark!

"The meeting didn't last long. I quickly learned that these self-styled 'gunslingers' had burned through our $500,000 investment in ninety days and were looking to me to replenish their bank account. I flew back to Pittsburgh and made the dreaded report to my Chicago partners, who confirmed what I expected. They had nothing more to contribute; neither money nor ideas about what to do. They were writing it off. I was on my own.

"A week later I was back in Dallas for a board meeting I had requested. Once convened, everyone looked at me, no doubt expecting a 'bail out.' Instead, I proposed that they elect me chairman and chief executive officer, and then they all resign effective immediately. 'Or else what?' one asked. 'Or else I get up and walk out,' I replied.

"There were murmurs of dissent, so I collected my papers and headed for the door. 'Where are you going?' 'Back to Pittsburgh,' I replied. A few minutes later, I was chairman and the sole director of TTI. On the flight back, I elected myself non-executive Chairman of Hovermarine Transport Ltd. It was the early spring of 1970. TTI's headquarters moved from Dallas to the bottom left drawer of my office desk.

"My first challenge was to find some operating capital. I had met a young banker with Chase Manhattan Bank called Tom Herlihy in New York City, and I went to see him. When I say 'young,' I thought I was young at thirty-two years; Tom looked as if he couldn't be much more than twelve! I was stunned to learn he had a $5 million lending authority. After an hour, I literally walked out of the meeting with a credit line of $200,000. I directed the funds to a fix for the HM2."

For the ride problem, a small team of Hovermarine engineers led by a young naval architect named Nigel Gee provided a solution, the bulbous bow. Using the same flexible neoprene material as for the bow and stern skirts, they extended the forward air cushion up to the edge of the main deck, and thereby created a shock absorber that deflected rogue waves. Ride characteristics and seaworthiness were measurably improved.

At the same time, another team, led by Managing Director Ed

Bill Zebedee, Eaon Furnell, and Ed Davison share some humor on the balcony in the Hazel Wharf plant

Davison and Eaon Furnell, were slowly but surely running down and correcting the mechanical flaws. Davison had been the leader of the General Dynamics team, and Zebedee had asked him to move to the UK when he became TTI's chairman.

What emerged by the beginning of 1972 was a reasonably seaworthy and reliable vessel, designated the 216. Four were sold that year, including the first of three craft purchased by Sociedade do Adoxe in Portugal.

HOVERMARINE

PART TWO

1973 – 1979

The Dominant Years

HOVERMARINE

CHAPTER THREE

BEGINNING A NEW BEGINNING

ZEBEDEE'S OVERNIGHT FLIGHT FROM Pittsburgh touched down on time at London Heathrow. With no checked luggage and nothing to declare for British customs, he breezed through and emerged to the crowd gathered around international arrivals. He was surprised to see Ed Davison, who greeted him warmly. His opening statement was, "Glad you're on schedule. We have just enough time to make it to London High Court for our hearing."

"What hearing?" Bill asked.

"Our eviction hearing," Ed replied. "Barings* have sued for vacant possession of our factory. We're due in front of the judge at 10:00 a.m."

They arrived at London High Court and checked the day's docket to determine their assigned courtroom. In the corridor, they were introduced to their Barrister, one Jeremy Blackett-Ord Q.C. After exchanging quick pleasantries, they were called to Court. Zebedee listened to the Baring Brothers* barrister, and thought he made quite a persuasive case that they were indeed trespassers.

Then Blackett-Ord rose from his chair, and after a theatrical pause for effect, he reached down to a glass and took a drink of water! Zebedee thought, *He hasn't a clue what to say!*

* For those who don't remember, Barings had been a prestigious merchant banker since the middle ages until the mid-1990s, when a rogue trader brought the whole firm down.

A few minutes later, after the judge had properly excoriated Blackett-Ord for wasting the court's time, he summarily dismissed Hovermarine with a thirty-day order to deliver vacant possession to Barings.

Bill continues: "A few days later, I was granted a meeting with Lord something-or-other at the Barings offices in the City of London. Of course, we were kept waiting for the best part of an hour, likely just to demonstrate that they were in control.

"Finally, his Lordship, along with an entourage of minions, made his entry. I made a point of seeming to ignore them, instead remaining seated and looking around the meeting room. After a momentary pause, his Lordship asked if I found the room not to my liking. Not at all, I replied, adding that I was merely wondering how many of our hovercraft they were going to be able to fit in the space. I explained that we could not afford to move them and had no place to put them, so Barings might want to consider what they would do with five boats having a cumulative length of 250 feet.

"A few weeks later, we signed a short term lease on the property known as Hazel Wharf. Shortly thereafter, in a dealing we were not privy to, Barings hived off the property to Czarnikow, a major London-based sugar merchant. We then entered into a long term lease with Czarnikow, which proved to be a far friendlier landlord, and Hazel Wharf became the home of HTL for the next thirteen years."

CHAPTER FOUR

1973: A YEAR OF TRANSITION

BILL ZEBEDEE CONTINUES: "After much legal posturing and negotiating, I bought the interest in TTI held by my erstwhile co-investor, and my investment company became the controlling shareholder. To say that I was 'in over my head' was a massive understatement! HTL had an enormous need for capital to develop and commercialize what was a promising technology but virtually no incoming revenue. There was only one possible solution...

"...a share offering to the public! And so I set about to sell the technology as the way of the future. I reasoned that I was quite good at selling 'blue sky' ideas, having at age thirty-one convinced a group of investors to give me a couple of million dollars to fund my venture enterprise.

"On 12th January 1973, TTI (renamed Hovermarine Corporation) sold 150,000 shares at $10 in a successful public floatation. Now it was time to produce results, not only to justify the faith my new shareholders had shown by their investment, but also to attract the vastly greater capital that I knew would be needed in the future."

As noted earlier, the first three 216s were purchased by a newly formed Portuguese company for ferry service in the Lisbon area. The company's managing director Agostino da Silva, was a savvy businessman, and the enterprise was successful from day one.

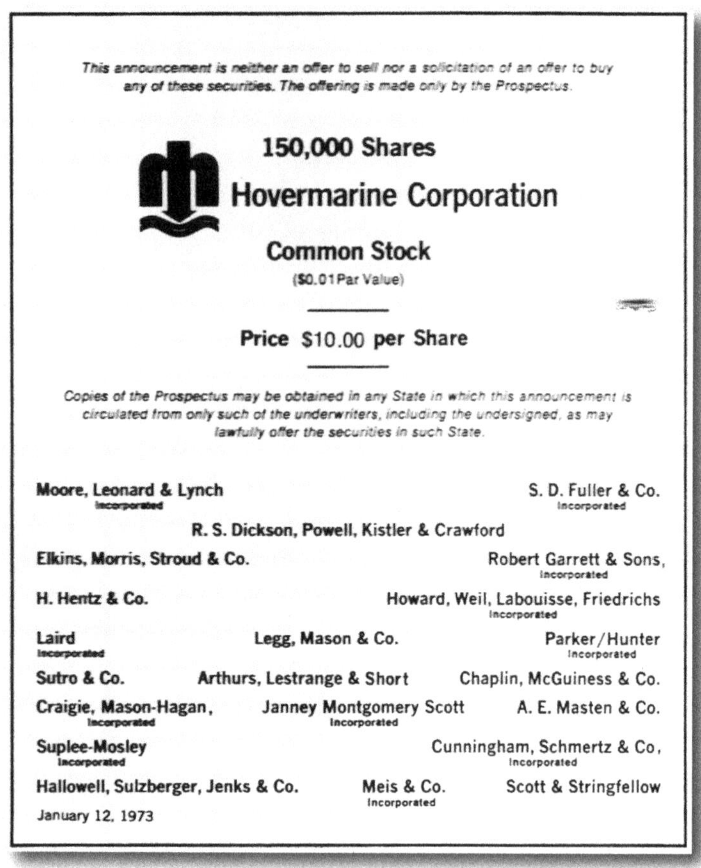

This announcement is neither an offer to sell nor a solicitation of an offer to buy any of these securities. The offering is made only by the Prospectus.

150,000 Shares

Hovermarine Corporation

Common Stock

($0.01 Par Value)

Price $10.00 per Share

Copies of the Prospectus may be obtained in any State in which this announcement is circulated from only such of the underwriters, including the undersigned, as may lawfully offer the securities in such State.

Moore, Leonard & Lynch Incorporated
S. D. Fuller & Co. Incorporated
R. S. Dickson, Powell, Kistler & Crawford
Elkins, Morris, Stroud & Co.
Robert Garrett & Sons, Incorporated
H. Hentz & Co.
Howard, Weil, Labouisse, Friedrichs Incorporated
Laird Incorporated
Legg, Mason & Co.
Parker/Hunter Incorporated
Sutro & Co.
Arthurs, Lestrange & Short
Chaplin, McGuiness & Co.
Craigie, Mason-Hagan, Incorporated
Janney Montgomery Scott Incorporated
A. E. Masten & Co.
Suplee-Mosley Incorporated
Cunningham, Schmertz & Co, Incorporated
Hallowell, Sulzberger, Jenks & Co.
Meis & Co. Incorporated
Scott & Stringfellow

January 12, 1973

Underwriters' traditional tombstone advertisement as appeared in *The Wall Street Journal* on January 12, 1973

The on-site HTL field service crew, led by Captain Bill Thwaites and chief mechanic Dudley "Robby" Roberts, were soon returning with very positive feedback. For a workforce that had suffered years of product failure and liquidation, the success of Portugal fed a sense of pride and accomplishment that quickly permeated the still small organization. This enthusiasm would spiral even higher when word came that daSilva was coming to Southampton to purchase three more craft.

Then disaster hit. Portugal, under the dictator Salazar, was lurching towards political crisis that would ultimately lead to revolution and the installation of a communist government. Da Silva was apparently on the wrong side of these politics, and arrested while boarding an airplane at Lisbon airport. He was never again heard from. The boat service eventually would be seized by the communists and ultimately fail.

For HTL, the disaster was compounded by the fact that the company, anticipating the order from Portugal, already had two of the three craft under construction with no immediate prospective buyers.

Back at the Hovcorp office in Pittsburgh, Bill Zebedee was coming to the realization that, unless somebody sold something very soon, both HTL and its parent company were heading towards bankruptcy. Yes, the company had sales leads, but almost all were unformed businesses, at best long term prospects. For Hovermarine, "long term" had become a matter of just a few weeks!

One name stood out on the HTL prospects list, the Hongkong & Yaumati Ferry Company (HYF). It was not only an established enterprise; it was the world's largest ferry company in terms of passengers carried. HTL's sales manager for the Far East, Graham Gifford, had been doggedly pursuing the account, but the customer was insisting on a demonstration in Hong Kong before placing an order. Clearly a demonstration was no answer to the urgent problem; someone had to force the issue.

Zebedee decided to visit Hong Kong.

HOVERMARINE

CHAPTER FIVE

HONGKONG & YAUMATI FERRY COMPANY

IN OCTOBER 1973, BILL flew to Hong Kong, accompanied by his wife. He realized this trip might well make the difference in the very survival of Hovermarine. Gifford was delighted that someone was finally paying attention to this deal, and was at Kai Tak airport to meet his flight.

The airplane landed around midnight local time. In his own words, Bill describes what followed: "I saw Graham as we exited customs, accompanied by a man that turned out to be our agent, Walter Sulke. Graham had previously told me Sulke was an old China hand who held the lucrative Mercedes Benz distributorship for the colony. Walter was evidently out to impress me, and his Grand Mercedes 600 limousine waited at the curb for the trip to our hotel. Enroute, there was small talk and then Sulke turned to the HYF prospects.

"He said he was very confident that the managing director, a man called Edmond Lau, was very serious about buying, but then came the punch line...Walter said the Chinese were always slow to warm up to Americans and Europeans, and so the deal was probably still two years in the future. I very nearly told him to turn the car around and return me to the airport—I had a payroll to meet!"

A meeting with the HYF directors was set for the following morning, and Bill knew, despite the urgency of his situation, it would be considered rude if he did not attend. As expected, the session was somewhat stiff and formal, but it was quickly established that the first hurdle would be approval by the Hong Kong Marine Department for HM2s to operate at speed (30 knots+) in a harbor where the speed limit was 8 knots. Mr. Lau had arranged a meeting with HKMD for that morning, and in due course the participants, Lau and three of his board plus Sulke, Gifford and Zebedee descended to street level to board the vehicles that would transport them to the meeting. It was there that what Zebedee would later describe as a seminal moment in Hovermarine history occurred.

Again, in his own words: "We were standing at the curb, and Mr. Lau asked me where I lived in America. I told him Pittsburgh and he said he had never been there, but had spent a lot of time in New Hampshire. I said I had also, and it must have been the expression of surprise on my face that prompted him to blurt out, 'You go to Dartmouth?'

"Not only were we both alumni of Dartmouth College and graduates from its business school, but Edmond had been only one year behind me. We bonded instantly! When he learned that my wife was with me, he immediately invited us for dinner that evening with his wife, Janet. The four of us would become very close friends, and over the next decade share many adventures in Hong Kong, China and elsewhere.

"With the ice thus suddenly broken, our meeting with HKMD turned into a tour de force for the HYF/Hovermarine 'team.' The authorities were concerned about the wash an HM2 at speed would create, and with the aid of a short movie I had brought along, we were able to show that the boat's wake was minimal. The matter was settled, and the officials assured us that they would approve HM2s for operation in all territorial waters.

"The following morning we reconvened with the HYF Board. Edmond announced that they were prepared to immediately purchase four craft, subject to two conditions; first was price and terms, and second was that the boats have air conditioning satisfactory to HYF's engineering department. With confidence I did not really feel, I assured them that air conditioning would be no problem. Price and terms were quickly agreed, and the lawyers were instructed to prepare contracts.

"I left the next day for previously scheduled meetings in Tokyo with our prospective partners in the joint venture that would become known as Hovermarine Pacific Ltd. It was agreed that I would return to Hong Kong in two days' time for contract signing, and in the meantime I left Graham Gifford and Walter Sulke to work through the legal details.

"Once on board the flight for Tokyo, I finally had the chance to take a deep breath and reflect with my wife on the whirlwind events of Hong Kong. First I had to acknowledge the extraordinary good fortune of being a Dartmouth graduate, and silently made a commitment to increase my future contributions to the College alumni fund. Second, I knew we needed to organize an immediate effort to design and install air conditioning. I drafted a telex on the subject during the flight and had my Tokyo hotel send it back to Ed Davison as soon as I had checked in. I had wanted no record to exist anywhere in Hong Kong that I was less than confident in our ability to make it happen!"

Air conditioning an HM2 had never been an issue. The English climate, as well as that of most of Europe, was such that there was little demand, and installations in the 1970's were relatively rare. Indeed, the weather in Southampton was such that cooling effectiveness would be nearly impossible to measure. During tests of candidate designs, it was necessary to use space heaters to drive up the cabin temperature.

Because of the urgency, Zebedee also instructed the just completed Hovcorp plant in Titusville, Florida to mount a parallel effort. The hot, humid climate there was similar to that of Hong Kong. Surely the Americans would have the expertise needed to design a working system even if the HTL engineers failed.

As design teams on both sides of the Atlantic accumulated failure after failure, Edmond became increasingly frustrated. In September 1974, he called Zebedee, who was forced to admit that his people had not solved the problem. "To Hell with air conditioning," said Edmond. "Just ship the boats and we'll make our own air conditioning." And so, in October 1974, the first of the craft was shipped from Southampton. The HYF team quickly fitted it with a simple and inexpensive but effective system, and in December HYF inaugurated the first ever hovercraft service in Hong Kong. It was an immediate success, and Edmond Lau was soon in the market to purchase additional craft.

Not that he was totally happy with the HTL design. He wanted ten feet added to the boats, which would raise capacity to ninety passengers. A year later the first sixty-foot craft, HYF 105, was delivered. HTL designated model 218; it was powered with larger GM Diesel engines that not only improved reliability and performance, but replaced the Cummins' Diesels in the model 216 that had been a source of complaints from HYF.

Lau also wanted a new raised wheelhouse design that would enable skippers to have a 360° view. The first of those, HYF 109, was delivered in early 1978. The design was then frozen, and Hovermarine would eventually supply a total of thirty HM2s to the ferry company.

It is hard to overstate the significance of the HTL/HYF relationship to Hovermarine. It provided the Southampton factory with a steady base of business that became the foundation for the company's ventures into non-ferry applications. It provided long term stability for the Hazel Wharf work force; it buoyed morale and became a primary engine for growth. More important, it combined engineering resources of a British team that all-to-often thought they were designing exotic airplanes with

HM216 (left) meets HM218 in Hong Kong Harbour. Photo courtesy Fast Ferry International

The greatest number of HM2s ever shown in a single photograph, with 21 nested at the HYF shipyard and a 22nd departing

a totally pragmatic Chinese team whose focus was on simple, reliable and low cost marine craft.

Perhaps most important, HYF gave Hovermarine a credibility and identity in the international marketplace. HYF was the world's largest ferry company. The scale of its operations was staggering; for example, it took in eight tonnes of money every day of the year from fares alone. Prospective Hovermarine customers were delighted to travel to one of the world's most exotic cities to see HYF's operations first hand, and to meet a Chinese team that was both enthusiastic and professional.

Later, HYF would become the first buyer of the 200 passenger HM5, but first, many adventures for Hovermarine lay ahead.

CHAPTER SIX

TECHNIQUES D'AVANT-GARDE (TAG) AND THE CÔTE D'AZUR

IN JULY 1974, MIKE Richards, HTL's Finance Director, was named Managing Director, replacing Ed Davison, who was transferred to the Hovcorp Pittsburgh offices and made President in charge of U.S. operations. HTL was still focused on completing the four craft order for HYF, the last of which was shipped in March 1975. The order book for the balance of the year was looking a bit thin. Once again, the company was visited by a stroke of good fortune.

In Mike's own words, "We were in advanced negotiations with a Cherbourg based travel company for the sale of two HM2s to operate a service from Nice along the French Riviera coast. Contract terms had been agreed, together with a payment schedule. However there were two major concerns. The purchasers were relatively inexperienced in ferry operations, and we doubted that they had the financial strength to qualify for needed financing from ECGD (See Appendix B).

"We were then contacted by Techniques d'Avant-Garde, who had been alerted to the proposed deal. They expressed a strong interest in taking over the route and operation. It fit perfectly with their avante–garde image; running a hovercraft service on the French Riviera. The company had been founded by a Syrian-born Saudi businessman, Akram Ojjeh, who was an intermediary in deals between Saudi Arabia and France, particularly arms sales. Whilst having no ferry experience, the one advantage TAG did have was seemingly unlimited funds.

"Discussions progressed quickly in early 1976 as TAG wanted to start the service for the tourist season. Of course, this dictated that the craft be 216s, already built or nearing completion. Outline terms were quickly confirmed, and I went to Paris to finalise the deal. I was aided by TAG's anxiousness to do the deal, and I wanted to maintain this negotiating advantage. I checked in for one night at the five star Georges V Hotel, just off the Champs Elysses, from where I was collected and driven to TAG's palatial offices in central Paris.

"Discussions were reasonably straightforward, but we needed the order and deposit urgently. I used the argument that we could not deliver the craft in time unless the deal was finalised immediately because one of the craft would have to be shipped from our plant in the U.S., the UK facility being so busy...

"In the event they agreed. The deposit was the full price for one craft, and I told them we would immediately initiate shipping arrangements. For reasons that were never clear, the funds came from a Dutch bank, but two days later the money was in our account, and we told Titusville to ship the craft."

Meanwhile, back in Pittsburgh, Bill Zebedee was delighted by the news of the TAG sale, and especially pleased that Mike Richards had been able to put the deal together by himself. For more than a year, Bill had been commuting between Pittsburgh and Southampton, spending three weeks at a time in each location. As he said on numerous occasions, "I was doing a great job for Trans World Airlines, but I was suffering chronic jetlag and doing a poor job for the company." He was contemplating a permanent relocation to the UK; perhaps that would no longer be necessary.

He was somewhat concerned that the deal had been put together virtually overnight and asked Mike for a copy of the contract. On reading it, he noticed a potential flaw; final payment (half the total contract value) was to be made after the second craft was delivered.

It is a cardinal rule in international commerce that all monies due be paid before the goods were given over to the buyer. Bill raised the issue with Mike, who assured him that payment would not be a problem. Since he had not met any of the TAG personnel, Bill deferred to Mike's judgement.

Zebedee was scheduled to travel to Tokyo for the first board meeting of Hovermarine Pacific Ltd. He and his wife would then stop in Hong Kong for preliminary talks on HYF's impending order for four more craft, and finally to the big island of Hawaii for holiday. Since his travel plans would overlap the planned delivery of the second TAG boat, Bill asked Ed Davison to go to Southampton for the specific purpose of ensuring that final payment was received before delivery.

Two weeks later, as he was checking into the Mauna Kea Resort, the desk clerk handed him a five-foot long telex from Davison. It had to be bad news...nobody sends long messages to convey good news!

Indeed, the French had taken possession of the second craft and were refusing to pay the balance due. Bill immediately started planning an early return to Pittsburgh, and sent Hovcorp's general counsel, Charles Cohen, a telex outlining the problem. He requested that Chuck arrange for a French-speaking lawyer from his Pittsburgh-based firm to be ready to travel to Europe as soon as possible.

In Bill's own words, "Upon my return from Hawaii, I collected the French speaking lawyer. We flew to London and spent a couple of days in Southampton, making onward arrangements. We arranged to meet the TAG people in Paris and then flew there, checking into the Georges V.

"The initial meeting did not go well. Some unctuous French general led their delegation. He started by saying that they had asked for a discount on the price, and now they were taking it. Two more unproductive meetings followed, with a French list of complaints about the boats growing each day. After five wasted days, our team returned to Southampton."

With negotiations going nowhere, the Hovcorp lawyers recommended bringing the U.S. Government into the case. It made sense. Max Bishop (a Hovcorp director), was a retired ambassador and long-time friend of then Secretary of State Henry Kissinger, and he took the lead. After laboriously working through the bureaucracy, Max determined that the Government would do nothing until it could be proven that the vessel had been built in the U.S. This was a bit tricky, since the contract was with HTL and the hull had been built at Hazel Wharf. The company was able to accumulate sufficient documentation for the State Department but then they concluded that the matter was a commercial dispute, and thus outside their purview. It was another dead end.

Along the way, Bill Zebedee was following through with his plans to relocate to the UK. The Pittsburgh offices were closed and the Titusville plant was sold. The Zebedee family took up full residency in December 1976.

Bill continues: "In early July 1976, Chuck Cohen called me from Pittsburgh and suggested we simply repossess the boat. Possession was nine points of the law, he said, and having the boat back would strengthen our position. He assured me that while the act might be unconventional, it would not be illegal. I discussed the idea with Mike Richards, and we decided to give it a try. We asked for volunteers, and Bill Thwaites, Dudley Roberts and a junior mechanic immediately stepped forward."

Mike Richards continued, "Our last report had been that both boats were tied up at a pier in Toulon, unattended and unguarded. The crew not only agreed to go, but were eager to get on with it. It seemed everyone in the company was anxious to strike back at the French!

"They left on a Saturday in mid-July. With the banks closed, we were not able to provide them much of a cash advance, which would prove problematic because of the need to purchase fuel several times enroute.

"They found the two craft moored together. The target American boat was nearly empty of fuel, so they siphoned fuel from the other boat, and Robbie went about looking for other sources. He had a sense of taste and smell for good Diesel fuel, and during the day on Sunday, with the port closed down, managed to scavenge enough to allow them to make their first intermediate stop.

"In the dead of Sunday night," Mike continued, "they slipped the moorings and, lights out, drifted out into the harbour. About at midpoint, the port authority challenged the unidentified vessel. Thwaites fired up the engines, hit the navigation lights, and the boat sped out of the harbour. They ran until they were nearly out of fuel, pulling into a small fishing village on the French coast on Monday afternoon.

"Bill Thwaites rang me that evening to report. He had identified a small branch bank in the village, and I promised to transfer funds to him first thing the following day. In the event, it was Wednesday before they were able to locally draw the cash, refuel and get underway.

"Our hurried and loosely formed plan was to get the boat out of French waters before TAG realized what we had done, and to head for the safety of Gibraltar, about 800 nautical miles SW of Toulon. Unfortunately, the French woke up sooner than we had anticipated.

"On Friday 23rd July, the front pages of the Paris newspapers screamed the headline 'Piracy'! The TAG people were evidently quite angry! Reports in the papers over the next several days were that they had chartered two high speed Bertram yachts, taken on board heavily armed security people, and were scouring the French coastline for their lost boat. Happily for us, they badly underestimated the distance the HM2 could travel, and were searching the wrong places.

"With the French on the hunt, we decided that the boat should only travel at night, making daytime stops in small coastal villages. We had no idea that the French had enlisted the help of the Spanish Armada (Navy), but fortunately we avoided ports where they had a presence.

"By Friday 13th August, we expected them to make Valencia, and I was in the office waiting for the call. Very cool, I heard Bill, 'Mike, we have a problem. We are under arrest, and I'm looking at a gun.' I told Bill I'd urgently contact the British Consul, and assured him I'd be in Valencia the next day.

"Bill Zebedee and I flew over on the Saturday, met with the UK Ambassador, secured the release of the crew, and arranged flights back to the UK.

"I then flew up to Paris on the Monday morning to meet with the lawyers representing us in the arbitration proceedings. A little early for the meeting, I checked into my hotel and as was the case in those days handed over my passport for submission to the authorities.

"Upon meeting the lawyers, I happened to mention my hotel registration and passport. They immediately told me to go straight back to the hotel, retrieve my passport, and get out of France! My name was on a list of people the French Authorities wanted to detain on charges of piracy. The list also had the names of the crew and Bill Zebedee.

"They also told me that the Piracy laws dictating the guillotine punishment had not been repealed—I think they were joking, but, I did as I was told, and was very relieved to get out of France!"

Meantime, Zebedee had returned directly to Southampton and called Chuck Cohen on Sunday. They decided that with an

American boat in the hands of the Spanish Armada, it was time to reengage the U.S. State Department. On Monday, 16th August, before Bill was able to contact Max Bishop, he received a call from Richards, by then in the Charles de Gaulle Airport departures lounge waiting to board his flight home.

"I rang Max," Bill recounted, "and he promised to get things moving promptly. The next day, I received a call from the chargé d'affaires of the American embassy in Madrid, and we arranged to meet in Valencia a few days later. He assured me that freeing the boat would not be a problem.

"We met in my hotel suite at the agreed time, and I briefed the diplomat on the situation. He recommended we set a meeting with the local Commandante of the Spanish Armada for the following day, and then instructed the Madrid Embassy to make the arrangements. He then described in English what he would tell the Commandante in Castilian Spanish.

"As he talked, I became increasingly alarmed. His formal diplomat-speak made it sound as if we might as well be starting World War III! I pointed out that the dispute only involved a fifty-foot boat worth $250,000; hardly enough to create an international incident. He told me this was standard phraseology in diplomatic circles, and that he didn't intend to waste time screwing around with some two-bit Spanish naval officer.

"He then asked me what we planned to do once the boat was returned to us. I told him we would proceed to Gibraltar and then arrange shipping back to the UK or America. He asked about our French pursuers, and I acknowledged they could be a problem. 'No worries,' he responded, noting that a task force of the U.S. Sixth Fleet was currently patrolling in the central Mediterranean, and they would escort our boat to Gibraltar. 'They don't have anything better to do anyway,' he added. I was stunned!

"The meeting the following day was conducted entirely in Spanish, but I knew what our Chargé was saying, and I could see that the Commandante was becoming very uncomfortable. Afterwards, the American told me that the officer needed instructions from headquarters, but there should be no problem, and asked that I ring him at the Madrid Embassy when the boat was ready to depart Valencia. He left and I returned to Southampton.

"In any event, there was a problem. The Spanish elected to hand the boat over to the French and the Chargé was suddenly absent; I was told he had been called back to Washington for consultations. Once again, we were back to square one."

Along the way, HTL had initiated arbitration under the rules of the International Chamber of Commerce, which was the dispute mechanism incorporated in the contract. Five years later, the arbitrators would hand down a decision that was at best a pyrrhic victory for HTL, ruling that TAG pay $250,000 for the boat, but that the parties absorb their own expenses. For HTL, arbitration fees, and expenses plus legal fees had amounted to more than the price of the craft.

CHAPTER SEVEN

NIGERIA

FROM THE START, IT seemed like a fertile market for Hovermarine. Nigeria, lying along the West Coast of Africa, has an extensive coastline and major concentrations of population in coastal cities, notably the country's capital Lagos. Even more attractive, the country is oil rich. There are some drawbacks, of course. The climate is dreadful. Infrastructure is woefully insufficient and backward. The greatest challenge is endemic corruption.

In 1973, Graham Gifford joined Hovermarine. Over the ensuing two years, he made three lengthy trips to the country. It should be noted most would consider that any trip to Nigeria lasting more than ten minutes would be considered lengthy! He focused mainly on the center of Nigeria's oil riches, Port Harcourt, without success. It seemed that the corruption and frequent overthrows of local leaders always spoiled any progress.

In 1976, Graham was transferred to The Philippines to open a Far East sales office. As fate would have it, Graham had recruited the man who would become his successor for the Nigerian market, one Herbert Snowball. Graham had met Snowball in 1972, then managing a pub on The Isle of Wight. He joined the Company around 1974. Some would say that Herbert was an unusual personality, but there might have been a tacit belief that one needed a bit of eccentricity to be successful selling hovercraft. In any event, when the decision was made to relocate Graham to Manila, Herbert took over the Nigeria territory.

Early on it was an inside joke that the company had sent a Snowball to Nigeria, but Herbert definitely took his job seriously. As Mike Richards would later recount, "After a time, the only way we could get him to come home to report was to cut off the money we were transferring to him for expenses."

No one doubted Herbert's enthusiasm, and what reporting he provided described multiple and ever larger deals he was pursuing. He was promoting various ferry services, including one from downtown Lagos to the airport. He also had discovered that the Nigeria Ports Authority had some issues with their fleet of small craft, and had persuaded them that Hovermarine had just the team of service personnel to help. He negotiated a contract for services, and HTL dispatched a team to Lagos, led by lead mechanic Dudley Roberts.

Bill Zebedee thought it was time he paid a visit to the country, and in late 1975 he invited Edmond Lau to join him, in the role of an international public transport expert. Edmond flew to the UK; visas and inoculations were arranged, and the two then flew to Lagos.

Later, Edmond observed to Zebedee that Herbert had a typically British colonialist approach to dealing with the 'natives'; given his Colonial Hong Kong background, it was hard to dispute Lau's view of Snowball. When they attempted to check into the Federal Palace Hotel, Herbert was true to form when it was found that there was no record of the reservations for either Lau or Zebedee. Another bribe (£200) and one room was found available for them to share.

The room was a disaster; dirty, no running water, no air conditioning—all the usual discomforts. Zebedee immediately instructed Herbert to get them reservations on the next available flight back to London!

The following morning, Snowball told them he had heard

about a new Holiday Inn that was close to opening, but didn't yet have its telephones connected. They immediately took a taxi to see it. It was indeed in pre-opening mode but obviously brand new, clean and it had working air conditioning. Better still, room rates were half those at the Federal Palace, and the clerk, an American, actually refused a bribe. There were, the clerk pointed out, a couple of problems—there was no hot water, and the lifts were not working. The only unoccupied rooms were on the 12th floor or higher! They reserved two rooms for a week, and on checking in were delighted to discover that the hotel restaurant, run by a visiting American team, was quite acceptable.

The following day, Herbert had scheduled a meeting with the country's Minister of Transport. The Minister and his entourage were immediately captivated by Mr. Lau, partly because of his somewhat amusing way of speaking (owing to a childhood affliction that left one side of his face permanently paralyzed), but more because of the authority with which he spoke on public transport. When Edmond announced that one of things he wanted to do during his visit was to go on safari and become a "yellow hunter," the Minister nearly collapsed with laughter!

Herbert then took them to the NPA yard, lying on the bank of a river, where they observed literally hundreds of small boats, the first-glance condition of which ranged from new to unsalvageable. Robbie and his HTL team were close to completing their survey of this fleet, and reported to Bill and Edmond that not even one of the boats was operational! Worse, Robbie said that any HM2 operation in country would have to be permanently staffed from the UK; he said the Nigerians were "hopeless." Finally, Robbie said he and his team had decided Lagos was so unpleasant that they didn't ever want to see the place again!

Snowball arranged more meetings in the following days, including a session with a man Herbert said would definitely be the next Prime Minister....a man, he said, "we can do business with." Security in his compound was heavy, with machine gun carrying guards everywhere. A couple of months later, it was reported that the man had been assassinated!

When Bill returned to Southampton, he extolled the beauty of the Holiday Inn and suggested that John Chapman, HTL's Director of Customer Service, visit to assure his people that Nigeria was not a place to avoid. The plan was to negotiate for a permanent block of rooms to house assigned personnel in the future. On John's second evening there, as he was waiting for the local Nigerian agent to collect him for dinner, the Holiday Inn suddenly became a most unattractive option.

The Inn lobby was an open air affair, a few steps above a circular driveway entry passing under a porte cochere. John had just taken a seat on one of the lobby couches when a large black sedan pulled up to the entrance. Two men emerged with machine guns and began raking the lobby area with a hail of bullets. John leaped the couch and got down behind it. The episode lasted only a minute, but the lobby was a mess, with dead and injured strewn everywhere. John retreated to a lift (by then they were working), went to his room, packed his bag and took a taxi straight to the airport. He spent nearly two days in the relative safety of the departure lounge before obtaining a seat on a flight leaving the country for a European destination; any destination as long as it was out of Nigeria!

Undaunted, Herbert Snowball soldiered on and a few months later his effort began to show signs of success. He needed a company director to help close the deal. When no volunteers came forward, the intrepid Mike Richards stepped into the breach, making his first trip in October 1976.

The team picks up the story:

Richards: "Lagos (Ikeja) International Airport was a shambles—disorganised and unbelievably hot—no air conditioning. It took forever to be processed, going through Health Control (if you didn't have a yellow fever injection you weren't allowed in), Customs and Immigration. Then there was an interminable wait for luggage, often with only one carousel for multiple flight arrivals. Apart from Immigration, it was necessary to ease each process with the appropriate lubrication in US dollars.

"Next the taxi. When one was finally hailed, a price had to be agreed in advance. Once en route, it was quite normal for the driver to stop to renegotiate. If you did not, he would threaten to unload you. (This was the case every time with every taxi in Lagos)."

Gifford: "Yes, I'm glad I mostly missed the Lagos experience. I always thought the action would be the Port Harcourt oil patch, which is where I concentrated. I must say it couldn't have been much above conditions in Lagos. I made three trips in 1975, each about a fortnight. I did visit the NPA in both Lagos and Port Harcourt, but I remember these as technical/operational meetings rather than as potential customers.

"I recall talking to an expat who assured me that all the equipment rotting alongside the road from the airport into town was abandoned equipment (brand new) that was imported purely to release the associated bribes! I would later wonder if our craft were actually used much in Nigeria or whether they fitted into the above category."

Richards: "Herbert Snowball was already in situ when I arrived. He was truly a one off! Totally convinced he would make a sale, he was unstoppable and simply would not take no for an answer. I believe the Lagotians came to like him; they certainly found his name amusing!

"I don't know how he put up with living in Lagos. It had

nothing to offer – lousy food, hot, dirty, dangerous, and whites were very much disliked. The Brits were particularly out of favour because after the Coup d'etat, we had allowed the deposed Prime Minister to come to the UK. It was truly a nasty place to stay.

"Herbert finally prevailed and we reached agreement to sell three HM2s. The negotiations were very tortuous, but we eventually agreed a price and contract. There was to be a formal signing by the Minister of Transport—the proposed purchase had been leaked, so there was a lot of publicity.

"That same evening I received a call from our agent to say that the contract would be presented for signature exactly as agreed, but the price had been increased by US$100,000. I would be told in due course where to send these monies."

Furnell: "At the time, I was truly envious of all of you that were travelling to exotic places around the world whilst I was stuck in the factory. I found great humour in some of your stories. Many nights over dinner, I would say to Joyce, 'you won't believe what I heard today,' but I never had a desire for first-hand experience in Nigeria."

Zebedee: "No question in my mind, Mike, that you and Herbert were a great team! The deal simply would not have happened without you. I was sure as Hell not going back! Not only did you finalise the deal, but you made another trip in early 1977 when the first boat was shipped to Lagos."

Richards: "I was in Lagos when it arrived. There was to be a significant delay to unload it as there were many freighters lying in the Roads ahead of ours. Herbert contacted the Minister's Office, and lo and behold, the next day we were off! The freighter Captain was very, very happy to have jumped the queue, and Herbert and I were invited aboard for lunch and drinks. As Herbert was a teetotal, I helped him out.

"There was a highly publicised official launch ceremony with loads of politicians, local dignitaries, and bag carriers. I was very happy to see Herbert receiving the acclamation he had so much earned.

"Crew training then commenced. Our captain Bill Thwaites and engineers, which included Dudley Roberts and Peter White, did an amazing job in adverse circumstances, not the least of which was lack of air conditioning—this time on the hovercraft. It was a major problem, and created working conditions that were almost intolerable."

Zebedee: "Face it, crew training was a myth! Our chaps operated and maintained the craft. Forewarned by Robby, we had included in the original contract a year of full service, meaning we would train the trainable but run the service. We calculated all the possible costs, bribes and premiums to be paid to our people, and then prior to submitting the bid, I insisted on doubling the amount. We still lost our shirt! When we bid for a second year, we redoubled the first year price and again lost money. We simply could not keep up with inflation and the galloping corruption.

"Oh, and then there were our crews. Once the regulars had learned how dreadful the conditions were, we kept raising their salary premiums to keep the operation staffed. We were offering salaries that were four times their normal wages—some were being paid more than Mike! And still there were few takers. We tried advertising in the Southampton Evening Echo for recruits, but that didn't work out very well either."

Furnell: "Yes, and you tried to get some of the lads from the shop floor to go out there. I must say I'm glad that didn't work out."

Wilkins: "You all know that I joined this party a bit late, but I remember we were having problems getting money transfers for our crews' expenses through the banking system. The fees on the Nigerian end were outrageous. We came up with a great scheme. I would purchase blocks of first class BA open tickets in the UK for passage from Lagos to London. The lads would then sell them locally for cash. It amazed me that there was a seemingly endless demand!"

Richards: "At some point we decided that we could no longer pay for Herbert to stay at the hotel, so he went native, and found lodging with a local lady. The last time I saw him was in 1979, on my last trip to Lagos. Essentially I decided then that there was no alterative but to simply walk away from the whole mess. We abandoned the boats, presumably to that huge NPA bone yard where all its purchases went to die. Fair to say that Herbert abandoned us and we never again heard from him."

Readers will note that the above conversation, which came out of a Zoom teleconference in early 2020, is missing Peter White, whose experience would prove to be our best record of what really happened in Nigeria. We hadn't located Peter at the time, but when we did, he provided a fresh view of events in Nigeria and many other places in the world of Hovermarine. Even better, he had kept diaries of his entire ten year employment with the company. His story, in his own words, appears in Book Two.

CHAPTER EIGHT

COMPETITION

WITH THE MOMENTUM OF HYF sales, selling high speed ferry boats was bit easier, but unfortunately there were few established ferry operators. Too often, the HM2 was a solution looking for problems, compounded by the fact that most of the prospective customers were start-up, undercapitalized and inexperienced operators.

On the positive side, there was little competition in the high speed ferry market. British Hovercraft Corporation offered several amphibious hovercraft models, including the giant SR.N4, but their price range and operating costs were never competitive with sidewall hovercraft.

Alan Blunden is a renowned authority on all forms of high speed ferries, and publisher and editor of *Fast Ferry International*. No one is more qualified to speak on the markets and competition. According to him, "Although most Italian and USSR hydrofoil production was sold to domestic operators, there was some success in export markets. Until the appearance of the HM2, the seventy-two-seat PT.20 from Swiss designer Supramar and built in Italy by Rodriquez had no high speed competition in that size range. More than half of the 44 PT.20s built during 1956-1969 initially went overseas. Many of these later returned to Italy, some entering service with the builder's operating company. Hitachi also built seventeen PT.20s but only three of these were exported from Japan."

Alan continues, "Although most USSR production entered service domestically or in Eastern Bloc countries, the 116-seat Kometa was designed with an eye on export markets and about thirty of the almost 200 built were 'sold' (dumped) in Western countries, particularly Greece, where some are still operating.

"I've always thought that the HM2 destroyed the market for the PT.20-size hydrofoil. After the first HM2 was launched in 1968, the Italians built only six. The production line of the replacement design, the RHS 70, totaled only ten, six for Italian Government operators and four for Red Funnel in the UK.

"Boeing introduced the Jetfoil in 1974. Unlike the Italian and Russian surface piercing hydrofoils, Jetfoils were fully submerged. It was a technological marvel, especially in its capabilities in heavier sea conditions, but with a price in excess of $10 million each there were few takers.

"The export market for larger hydrofoil designs virtually disappeared when catamaran ferries appeared in the early 1970s. The first ones were marginally slower than hydrofoils but they were cheaper to buy (even from Norwegian builders!) and to maintain. Within a few years, there was no difference in the service speeds, and today the fast catamarans dominate the market."

By far, Jetfoil's largest operator was Shun Tak, controlled by casino magnate Stanley Ho, for the Hong Kong—Macau route. Shun Tak was the launch customer for the Jetfoil, it ordered two but these were the only new ones delivered to it by Boeing. The company eventually owned sixteen (two that Boeing had previously leased to several operators, six that arrived from Europe, three from Hawaii, two from Venezuela and one from Japan).

Today, Shun Tak, renamed TurboJet when Ho relinquished control, operate a mixed fleet that currently consists of seven Jetfoils, ten FBM Marine 45m catamarans, seven Austal 47.5m catamarans, three Fjellstrand 40m catamarans and two Fjellstrand FoilCat 35m hydrofoil catamarans. Only two, the FoilCats, were new when they were acquired by Shun Tak.

The Boeing Jetfoil

In 2007 a second company, Cotai Water Jet, backed by a rival Macau casino owner, started a competitive service, acquiring a fleet of fourteen Austal 47.5m catamarans over the ensuing two years. In February 2020 both fleets were laid up due to Covid-19 restrictions.

For reasons that were never clear, Edmond Lau started a service in 1983 to compete with Shun Tak. Named Sealink Ferries, Edmond purchased four new 200 passenger HM5s. Against the financial and marketing power of Stanley Ho and his large fleet of fast ferries, the company never stood a chance.

The only real competitor to Hovermarine's HM2 would turn out to be someone from "inside our own tent"; an HM2 operator who would start a company called International Catamarans.

In 1973, Graham Gifford had achieved his first Hovermarine sale, HM2 "Blue Dolphin," to Dolphin Ferries, owned and operated by Bjarne Halvorsen. Graham recalls, "Bjarne was a Norwegian-Australian whose brothers had established a virtual monopoly of ferry operations throughout Australia. Bjarne was a fairly droll, laconic individual who had built his house with his own hands on a magnificent site overlooking Sydney harbour. He also found time to be the Manager of the Australian Rugby Union team, the Wallabies.

"As for Dolphin Ferries, it was soon apparent that passengers were a major inconvenience. Bjarne was an excellent organizer and technical man but forgot about the customers! Whereas the routes were ideal for the craft, there was virtually no promotion or marketing of the services and after a couple of years the operation became untenable."

In 1976, a Tasmanian called Robert Clifford purchased the used Blue Dolphin craft and transferred it from Sydney to Hobart. For the next two years, it provided fast ferry service while the Hobart Bridge was being rebuilt. Thereafter, Clifford sold the craft to a New Zealand buyer.

According to Alan Blunden, "If there had been no Hovermarine, there might never have been an International Catamarans.

"Robert Clifford's thoughts about his 216 appeared in *Incat: The first 40 years*, a book he authored in 1998. In it, he recalls. 'The 64 passenger, British-built hovercraft was an instant success with the general public—twice as fast and twice as comfortable as the standard boats—but oh what a troublesome contraption! So troublesome, in fact, that three-quarters of all company maintenance activity had to be expended on one-quarter of the fleet and all for sixty-four people. With all its faults, however, it was very popular and stimulated thoughts of what we could do to make fast marine transportation better. It was number thirty-four off the production line, and I thought, if the English can sell thirty-four heaps of rubbish like this, how many properly engineered fast ships could we sell from Tasmania?...and so we started in the fast ferry business.'"

International Catamarans would become a very successful enterprise, licensing its designs around the world, including to two American companies.

However, by the mid-1970s Hovermarine was on a roll.

CHAPTER NINE

OTHER FERRY OPERATIONS

EARLY SUCCESS WITH THE HM2 series had allowed Hovermarine to gain momentum in the fast ferry marketplace, and to build its sales organization. The order book was soon growing. Some of the more notable operations are described below.

BOLIVIA

At first glance, Bolivia does not look to be much of a market. It is squarely in the Andes mountain range. Its capital, LaPaz is 10,000 feet above sea level. It had one tourist attraction, Lake Titicaca, elevation 12,500 feet, which borders Bolivia and Peru. The lake is 118 miles long and 45 miles across at its widest point. The scenery is spectacular, but tourist amenities were primitive. Conventional ferries and native reed boats had been tried, with limited success. The problem was that slow boats were just that; slow!

The lake was made to order for an HM2. It could tour most of the length of the Titicaca and return in six hours, making it a single day outing for tourists staying in LaPaz. At 30 knots, the scenery was constantly changing.

And there was a customer prospect, an entrepreneurial Bolivian national named Antonio Ossandon, who was already en-

Reed boat on Lake Titicaca

gaged in tourism. There was just one problem—how to get an HM2 from sea level at the port of Lima, Peru to the lake. Bill Zebedee assumed the problem could be solved by a heavy-lift helicopter, and so a single craft contract was signed with delivery f.o.b. Puno, Peru, on the west shore of Titicaca.

Bill soon learned that no helicopter is capable of operating above 10,000 feet; the atmosphere is just too thin. There was only one aircraft that could deliver an HM2 to LaPaz, from which the road was suitable for truck transport up to the Lake— the giant C5A, operated by the U.S. Air Force. Zebedee hoped that there might be some U.S. government program that would underwrite the cost, and asked Ambassador Max Bishop to investigate. Max soon came back with the direct telephone number for the commanding officer of a C5A squadron, somewhere in Illinois. Ed

Davison made the call, explaining to the general's chief of staff that we wanted to transport a hovercraft to Lake Titicaca.

"You want to transport a WHAT to WHERE?" came the incredulous reply. "Is this some kind of April fool's joke?" Once assured that the inquiry was serious, the officer provided a "ballpark" quote: $500,000 to pick the boat up in Houston, Texas, and fly it to Bolivia, and no, there would be no government subsidy to cover the cost.

Zebedee sent the Ossandon a telex stating that the company was unable to arrange delivery, and was surprised by the reply which indicated that the customer would accept delivery f.o.b. Lima.

Before shipping the boat from Southampton to Lima, HTL took out all the heavy components such as the three Diesel engines, radar, and tables and seats (the interior had been configured to accommodate forty passengers), crating it all for separate shipment. Even then, what remained weighed nearly eight tonnes.

What followed would surely be the most exciting delivery of an HM2 ever undertaken, entirely orchestrated by Tony Ossandon and assisted by three HTL field service people. The craft was unloaded at Lima and placed standing on one side on a flatbed trailer. Ossandon had arranged for a new Volvo lorry, and Volvo hired a local film crew to record the journey for promotional purposes.

There was something of a road leading up most of the way to the Lake; much of it had been cut in the sides of mountains years earlier for the purpose of hauling heavy generators to the lake. A cargo measuring 50' long, 20' wide and 12' high was quite a different proposition! There were turns and switchbacks in the road that were impossible to negotiate, and many times almost half of the boat would be out over the edge of a cliff.

For the impossible transits, Ossandon had arranged a crew of some 300 indigenous Indians, who literally manhandled the boat off the flatbed and carried it up mountains. The trip took nearly a fortnight, but the boat was soon reassembled at Puno, and made its way to the Bolivian shore. The service was an instant success, leading Ossandon to purchase a second craft.

In late 1977, Peter White was sent to Bolivia, loaded down with boxes of Hovermarine spare parts, including a full set of Hovercraft skirt segments. In the terminal building and before customs, he was met by Tony Ossendon. All the bags and spare parts were whisked through customs, without doubt helped along by bribes. As they left the Airport Peter noticed a giant billboard by the roadside with a picture of the HM2 skimming across the lake passing some traditional Inca reed boats.

The major problem with the Bolivian operation was political. Bolivia had had 180 presidents during its first 170 years of existence. Revolutions and Coups were a common occurrence, and whenever there was a coup the tourists would stop coming. Once things settled down the tourists would slowly return, but the trade was not sufficient to make operating the hovercraft profitable.

Finally, political instability killed the operation, forcing a shutdown. The government that seized power in 1971 managed to hang on until 1978, but by 1977, turmoil had virtually killed tourism. Ossandon was unable to service the loans from ECGD.

Not wanting the company's record with ECGD to be blemished by a default, in 1978 Roderick Wilkins was sent to LaPaz with a view to negotiating a revised payment schedule. Rod recounts what would be the final chapter of the Hovermarine experience in Bolivia:

"Two or three days after I arrived, the day before we were due to meet with Ossendon, there was a coup d'etat and the streets filled with teenage soldiers with AK47s, chewing coca leaf and fingering their triggers uneasily. The British Embassy sent a minibus to collect us from the hotel on an hour's notice and take us to the airport, where they put us on the next flight out to a place called Guyaquil in Ecuador. After that we were on our own to figure out how to make it home the rest of the way. I never did get to meet Ossendon.

"Some two years later, I flew to LaPaz to assess the chances of putting the deal back together. I arrived just in time for another coup! I believe that time Ossandon must have backed the wrong side, and he had been declared persona non grata. To my knowledge, he was never heard from again. Subsequently, we tried to interest a Peruvian group, but they were unable to raise any capital. I am certain the HM2s were abandoned up on the lake."

BATAAN – MANILA OPERATION ("BATMAN")

Publicity about the opening of the HYF HM2 service created some new sales leads in the region in early 1975, one of which was Manila. While with BHC, Graham Gifford had become acquainted with Colonel Ramon and Gabby Zosa, and now he found they had purchased a Russian hydrofoil for a tourist route between Manila and Bataan, but had quickly concluded that the hydrofoil was unreliable. It was powered by a Diesel engine designed for a Soviet tank (Zebedee noted that U.S. Army studies showed that the average life of a tank engine in battle was fifteen minutes!). Worse, the Russians made spare parts according to a rigid five-year plan. Once the inventory of any part was exhausted, the customer might have to wait months or years until the next plan was implemented.

Colonel Zosa was an ex Philippines Air Force pilot and a Philippines Airlines Captain. His plan was to run high speed HM216s in place of his hydrofoil, from the newly built Imelda Marcos Shopping and Conference Centre in Manila across the Bay thirty miles to the island of Corregidor, and then on to Mariveles in Bataan Province. The island guarded the entrance to Manila Bay, and had been heavily fortified by the Spanish in the 16th century and by the Americans since 1903. Its strategic position had played a major role in the invasion and liberation of the Philippines in World War II, and was potentially a major tourist attraction, particularly for American and Japanese visitors.

The Zosa family were close to Ferdinand and Imelda Marcos,

which in the 1970s was essential to operating any business in The Philippines. The deal was perfect for Hovermarine! There was the problem of what to do with the Russian craft, but Bill and Graham dealt with that by arranging a trade-in. It worked, not only clinching the deal, but serving as a marketing tool for other operators looking to trade up other assorted ferries around the world.

With the expanding business in the Far East, the draw of customer prospects to HYF and the formation of the Hovermarine Pacific joint venture in Japan, Zebedee decided it was time to establish a presence in the region. From an expense standpoint, Hong Kong and Tokyo proved out of the question, but Manila seemed perfect. He asked Graham, who had become quite close with the Zosa family, to take up a position with Hovcorp and relocate. In late 1975, the Giffords, Graham, Geraldine, and their two children, moved from UK to a rented home in an expat section of Manila.

Graham picks up the narrative: "Shortly after we arrived in Manila, beautiful young Filipinas were being recruited as cabin crew, and the first aid and lifesaving training was carried out in our small swimming pool! Colonel Zosa had set high standards for staff training, and he demanded the service operate very professionally."

Peter White made his first trip for Hovermarine in August 1976. Two craft were already operational. The third was offloaded in Manila three months after Peter's arrival.

He recounts, "Manila Bay was full of debris which presented a constant problem, particularly for seawater intakes, propellers and skirts. On one occasion whilst crossing the bay the craft hit some debris that broke an attachment of the rear air cushion seal. We were stranded twenty miles from base. Our valiant Filipino seaman and appointed diver went over the side and we attached some ropes to the loop and hauled it up onto the aft deck. We were amazed that we were then able to increase speed to almost normal cruising speed even with a major part of the air cushion system missing.

"Time after time, incidents like this helped to build my confidence in what was turning out to be a most durable and well-designed vessel."

When the seas in Manila Bay were calm, the 216s excelled, but there were too many times when the waves exceeded three feet. The ride then became uncomfortable and the journey time, usually one hour, was significantly lengthened. Gradually, the craft load factor diminished and the operation was wound up.

TURISMO MARGARITA, VENEZUELA

In 1975, Hovermarine received an inquiry from a man called Kenny Delgado in Caracas, who was trying to establish a ferry service between the northeastern coast of Venezuela and Isla Margarita in the Caribbean Sea, a distance of twenty-five miles. After written communications and a preliminary feasibility study, Delgado announced that he would like to visit Southampton. The mere fact that he would pay his own expenses for the trip elevated him to the serious prospects list!

Delgado was young and without relevant experience, but he represented a "Workers' Bank" in Caracas that would provide full financial and management backing for the enterprise. Since Bill Zebedee was still resident in Pittsburgh and thus closer geographically, he arranged to fly to Caracas. He met the Bank President, who introduced Bill to a translator to be assigned to him for the entirety of his stay. And what a translator! She was young, stunningly beautiful, 100% fluent in both Spanish and English and very smart. Within a couple of days she was translating Bill's thoughts into Spanish even before he spoke them in English. She was also the bank president's daughter.

The deal was quickly completed, and two HM216s were soon on the way to Venezuela.

Bill and his wife attended the inauguration of the service. The trip to the island took only one hour, and was very pleasant. A celebratory luncheon was held for the invited guests and local island dignitaries, and the guests boarded for the return trip to the mainland. About halfway along it became obvious that an HM216 was no match for the suddenly changing sea conditions of the open Caribbean. Nearly everyone was seasick and the skipper, navigating solely by radar, wandered off course. After three hours, the boat made landfall on a remote part of the coast, and finally limped back to its port well after dark.

The company, Turismo Margarita, tried to make a go of the service, but sea conditions were such that frequent cancellations were necessary. However, the HM2s had proven that there was a real market for high speed service to the island, and the bank then purchased two Boeing Jetfoils for $20 million. The high-tech Jetfoils easily handled the sea conditions, and the service gained early success.

Sadly, it would end in tragedy. One of the Jetfoils struck a whale, literally knocking it out of flight and plunging it from 40 knots to dead stop in a few feet. Several passengers sustained serious injury, and the cabin attendant, serving drinks, was hurled into the forward bulkhead and died of her injuries. She was the bank president's daughter.

Boeing immediately sent a team from Seattle to investigate the accident. Ultimately, it was concluded that the underwater sound of the gas turbine engines and the massive waterjets that propelled the craft mimicked a whale's mating call. The incident would prove to close off the market for further Jetfoil sales, except for the Hong Kong to Macau service, which is where the Venezuelan Jetfoils would end up.

HM5 AND SEALINK FERRIES

From the early 1970s Hovermarine had ambitions to scale up its HM2 to a larger model, a 200-passenger version capable of operation in higher sea states. The concept was designated HM5, but lack of financial resources prevented any serious work to turn it into reality. By 1976, with Edmond Lau pushing for craft with greater capacity and with its own stronger financial situation, HTL undertook the first concrete steps towards producing a finished product. When Hovercraft Development Limited offered to support the design and development, work began in earnest.

In retrospect, from its earliest conception the HM5 was doomed to failure, for three reasons. First, its underlying assumption was that sidewall hovercraft was a fully developed technology, and no real attempt was made to advance that technology, nor consider alternatives. Second, its design virtually precluded adaptation to non-ferry applications. Finally, there was still a preponderance of aircraft design thinking within Hovermarine; it would have been better had the Chinese pragmatists from HYF been involved in the design process from the start.

The prototype hull was completed by early 1979 and moved to the newly acquired Solaris factory. Responsibility for outfitting and trials was assumed by Vosper in the beginning of 1980, and the completed craft was launched in early 1981.

Meantime, as noted earlier Edmond Lau had formed a new company called Sealink to open a route between Kowloon and Macau, and in late 1981, Sealink ordered four HM5s.The first, named Tejo, was delivered in 1982. It did not start well. Shortly after its arrival, Sir John Rix, by then Chairman of Vosper Hovermarine Ltd, received an angry call from Edmond Lau, and he dispatched Eaon Furnell to Hong Kong to address Edmond's concerns.

Eaon picks up the narrative: "When I arrived I got both barrels from Edmond, saying we were in danger of affecting his planned launch of the new service to Macau. I then met on the boat with their engineering team and was quite embarrassed with some of the obviously shoddy workmanship. It was clear to me that our on-site service engineer needed help. I phoned Robert Ducane, then VHL's MD, to send Robby and Brian Rowland from the Vosper design team. Ducane gave me the excuses on cost of flights, hotels etc. A call to Sir John and they were on their way.

HM501 *"Tejo"* undergoing sea trials in the Solent

"Robby soon sorted out the production snags, and Brian satisfied their issues on the design faults. Bill Zebedee then came to Hong Kong and Edmond calmed down, but at the wash up meeting, Edmond had another go at me, I think to impress his team. He later took me on a trial run to Macau and gave me a quick look around the casinos there. On the way back he thanked me and said how happy he was with our effort, which would enable him to meet his new service deadline."

However, by then both HM5s and Jetfoils were suffering significant passenger traffic losses. The bigger and less expensive high speed catamarans were taking over.

Alan Blunden remains a keen observer of the Hong Kong-Macau market, and picks up the story. "I was always puzzled by Sealink Ferries. One reason for its launching may have been that the Portuguese government would only award casino licenses to companies that were already operating ferries to Macau.

"At the time, it was reported that HYF owned 12.5% of the

HM503 *"Sado"* after being painted in its new Hong Kong Ferry livery

company but Far East Hydrofoil (Shun Tak) also owned 8.33%. By the end of 1984, HYF had become the largest, but not the majority shareholder. It seems that Sealink Ferries' plan had been that it would be the only company operating between Kowloon and Macau, but Far East Hydrofoil and Hongkong Macao Hydrofoil were both also given licenses for the route. Both Sealink and HMH struggled to compete with FEH. In 1987, Sealink operations were closed down.

"In 1989, the four HM5s were transferred to Hong Kong Ferry (as HYF was restructured that year) and they continued in service on the Macau route until they were replaced by catamarans in 1993. They remained on the domestic Hong Kong-Tuen Mun route and also replaced HM2s between Kowloon and Shekou. When New World First Ferry won the Hong Kong Government tender for domestic routes in 1999, HKF leased all four HM5s for one year while new catamarans were being built. They were then laid up."

THE UBIQUITOUS 485

In 1983, Vosper Hovermarine sold HM218 485 to British Technology Group, the successor to the Crown Corporation Hovercraft Development Ltd. The craft was initially leased to Sealink UK, named Ryde Rapide, and operated for three months during the summer of 1983 between Portsmouth and Ryde.

The following year it was leased to Harbor Bay Maritime for fifteen months. This operation, in San Francisco Bay under a temporary waiver of the Jones Act, is covered in detail in Book Two.

The next lease, for six months in 1989, was to Hovertransport in Norway, who operated a service along Oslofjord. The delivery trip from Southampton is also described in Book Two.

During 1992-1997, 485 was based in Palma, Spain, but went to sea very rarely. In 1997, it was sold to an American company that planned to introduce a service in Sierra Leone. 485 left Palma in mid June on an eventful 3,730 nautical mile delivery voyage to Freetown, where it eventually arrived the following March. The trail then went cold.

HM218 485, purchased by British Technology Group and first leased to Sealink UK

HM218 485 at Woolston Works following its repainting for Harbor Bay

THE AMBASSADOR'S WIFE INCIDENT (*BY MIKE RICHARDS*)

It had started so well! For a very long time we had been trying to sell craft into South Korea, but had made little headway. The breakthrough we had hoped for came when the South Korean Ambassador to the Court of St James accepted an invitation to visit our plant for a tour, and ride on an HM2 hovercraft.

We needed to impress; South Korea had a development programme, and we wanted to be part of it!

The day duly arrived, and we were to do it in style. Two chauffeured Bentleys were hired for Ted Tattersall (Technical Director) and me to be taken to the South Korean Embassy in Palace Gate London, where we would collect His Excellency Dr. Pyo-Wouk Han, his wife Madame Han and entourage.

From the embassy we proceeded uneventfully to our facility in Southampton, where the rest of the directors, their wives, and other guests were waiting to meet us. After coffee and cakes, the ambassador and his party were given a tour of the facility (well received) prior to the highlight—the hovercraft trip.

We proceeded to the pier, and then it all went horribly wrong!

To embark the craft there was a gangway that needed to be negotiated leading from the pier down to the pontoon where the craft was tied. Due to the state of the tide, the drop was around twenty feet, making the gangway quite steep. Further, the weather was typical of February in England, driving rain, very cold, with a gusting wind blowing in from the Solent.

Shortly after embarkation had begun, there was suddenly a loud splash, followed by noisy confusion. I got to the edge of the pier, looked down and saw a woman lying face down, prone in the water. No choice but to jump in! Having got her to the side of the pontoon, she was pulled out. I then realised it was Madam Han, the ambassador's wife!

The water was extremely cold, and Madame Han was clearly overcome by the shock. An ambulance was urgently called, and she was rushed to hospital accompanied by one of her aides.

Unfortunately, we had invited the Press along to join the tour and to ride with us on the craft, the idea being they would take pictures and report favourably on our efforts to export hovercraft. This would be good publicity. Instead they took pictures of a bedraggled lady being hauled from the water and dragged up a gangway, closely followed by me, a very wet, disconsolate managing director!

To add insult to injury, the Press considered this potential drowning much more interesting than a ride in a hovercraft, so they left immediately with their pictures to file copy in time to be printed in the evening and daily papers, where it made the headlines.

After his wife had left for the hospital, the Ambassador, a diplomat to the core, did make the hovercraft trip, following which he was whisked off together with his entourage and the Hovermarine group for lunch at a local hotel.

In the meantime, I had returned home for a shower and

Daily Mail, Monday, FEB 6 1978

Ambassador's wife falls into river

A helping hand for Mrs Han as the steps back on to dry land after her river plunge.

By FRED WEHNER

DIPLOMATIC silence yesterday enveloped an embarrassing incident in which the wife of South Korea's ambassador to the Court of St James found herself in a chilly English river.

Mrs Ghumgilion - Ghan Han, recovering in hospital from her ducking, wouldn't say a word about it.

Her husband, Dr Pyo-Wouk Han, wasn't talking either.

And the Englishman who dived in and pulled her out was keeping quiet, too.

Dr Han, his wife and a party of South Korean officials had gone down to Southampton as guests of Hovermarine, builders of Hovercraft, to see the factory and inspect the products.

Suddenly there was a splash, and Mrs Han was no longer expressing polite interest in Hovercraft, nor in their possible usefulness for her country's development programme.

She was way below, struggling in the ten foot deep River Itchen, fast-flowing, muddy and cold.

Hovermarine's managing director, Mr Michael Richards, plunged down the 20-foot bank and pulled her out.

An ambulance took Mrs Han to Southampton General Hospital. 'She had a very nasty experience and was badly shocked,' said a hospital spokesman.

'She is as comfortable as can be expected. We are keeping her in for a few days.'

But what actually happened?

'The Ambassador does not want his wife to talk about it, and nor will he,' said the hospital.

Dr Han was still maintaining his silence when he returned to his home in Parkside, Wimbledon, after visiting his wife.

Hero Mr Richards, of Harestock Road, Winchester, was unavailable for comment.

change of clothes. I kept thinking *How could this have happened? Clearly the gangplank was not fit for purpose...but we'd had no previous incidents...it was very windy...the Ambassadors wife was diminutive...what if we were sued....the adverse publicity....*

My mood was not improved at all when our manufacturing director Eaon Furnell rang to ask if I had enjoyed my swim!

Having changed, I went to the lunch venue, entering from the rear, hoping to arrive unnoticed; instead I was spotted, and given a round of applause. This was embarrassing.

The ambassador was chauffeured to visit his wife in hospital thence back to London. Ted Tattersall and I felt it appropriate to remain in Southampton!

Unfortunately the aggravation was not over. The Press had got wind of the story and were desperate to obtain more details, or an interview. However I had decided to make absolutely no comment about the incident. It could only make a bad situation worse.

The ambassador similarly refused to respond to any newspaper calls.

We visited Madam Han in hospital over the next couple of days, and thankfully she did make a full recovery.

A few weeks afterwards, Marian and I were invited to the Korean Embassy in London, where we were greeted by the Ambassador and his wife. I was presented with a plaque, and Marian was given a present. Cue more embarrassment! We were then their guests for lunch at the Ritz.

Later on that year we accepted an invitation to attend to a formal reception, held annually at the embassy. But again, this proved quite awkward; in conversations with other guests - members of the embassy, Korean businessmen and diplomats, I was asked how I had come to know the ambassador. When I explained the circumstances, I was once more embarrassed. Apparently the incident had been widely reported in the Korean press where it said I had saved the ambassador's wife from drowning.

Our invitations in the following years were politely declined.

We never did sell any hovercraft to South Korea!

Private award ceremony for Mike Richards, HTL Managing Director. *L to R*: Mike, his wife Marian, Madame Han and Ambassador Pyo-Wouk Han

HOVERMARINE

CHAPTER TEN

A STROKE OF GOOD FORTUNE

BY LATE 1977 HOVERMARINE was facing an overwhelming problem. Its burgeoning order book had completely outstripped the capacity of the 35,000 sq.ft. Hazel Wharf factory and the prospect of compounding the dilemma with construction of the first HM5 hull was absurd. It would be akin to giving birth to an elephant in a public telephone call box!

One morning John Hawking rang Bill Zebedee. Hawking was manager of the Woolston Branch of Lloyds Bank. His normal company contact was Mike Richards; the two had previously arranged a small borrowing facility, and Bill thought it was odd that "The Hawk" as he was known within HTL was calling him. Of course, he took the call.

Hawking immediately sounded as if he was a bit ill at ease. He hesitantly explained that the bank had a rather large borrowing relationship with Solaris Marine, and now found that they must put the company into liquidation. This would mean making its 125-man workforce redundant just before the Christmas holidays, which was bound to have an adverse effect on the bank's public image. John said he was wondering if Hovermarine might be interested in intervening, adding that the bank would be enormously grateful.

It had to be gift straight from Heaven! The Solaris factory was just further up the Itchen. The two properties were separated only by a lumber yard and a distance of perhaps 100 yards. It

The Hazel Wharf factory (circa 1979). Two HM2s being framed in the foreground, an HM501 in the upper left. Two Maraven and a Rotterdam craft are seen in the upper center. A tight fit!

River Itchen and Hazel Wharf (foreground). Part of the Solaris factory is visible in the upper left

had been famous in World War II as the Supermarine Spitfire Works; now some thirty years later, time had not been kind, but it was more than three times the size of the Hazel Wharf plant. It had four walls, a concrete floor and a roof, albeit leaky. Solaris had an extra bonus—125 experienced employees at a time Hovermarine were trying to recruit new workers. Zebedee quickly assembled a team to stroll up the road for a look.

Solaris/Supermarine plant following a repainting by Vosper

Solaris was not without its problems. Various versions of yachts were under construction and production was chaotic. Most issues were financial—Lloyds Bank was owed some £400,000 and fifty-odd suppliers were clamoring to be paid. While Eaon Furnell analyzed the shop floor problems, Bill and Mike Richards tackled finances.

The creditors never stood a chance against these two financial "engineers!" They soon had a package to convert the Lloyds' debt to a mortgage, and to take the company through a prearranged liquidation to "cram down" a forced settlement with the unsecured creditors. Given the bank's offer of gratitude, Zebedee threw in an additional loan request of £200,000. They even made a trip to Salisbury to gain approval from the Lloyds

Regional General Manager, Hawking's boss, with authority over more than 400 branches. What could possibly go wrong?

A few days later, a thoroughly embarrassed Hawking rang to report that the bank had turned down the deal! Zebedee was outraged, and pushed for an explanation. The Hawk explained that his Regional Manager had only a £400,000 loan limit, and so the decision had been pushed up to London. Although totally against protocol, John reluctantly gave Bill the name and telephone number of the responsible director.

Bill rang immediately and the man finally came on the line. His opening line was, "You Yanks are all the same. You never take no for an answer. I'm not even supposed to be talking to you."

Bill responded that he understood the bank's position, but that the Director might think about what he would say to the press later in the day, following HTL's announcement that they were immediately terminating negotiations, leaving Solaris with no choice but to liquidate and make all 125 employees redundant just in front of Christmas. It was a short conversation.

Hours later, Hawking rang to say that the bank had reversed its position and were ready to proceed with the deal.

Eaon Furnell and his team then worked miracles to reorganize production and integrate the two companies. However, it quickly became apparent that the yacht business was a loser. Bill would observe later that yacht building was the worst business he had ever encountered! Three incidents are worth recalling.

The main Solaris product was a 42' catamaran motor sailor with a list price of more than £100,000. The boat was popular on the continent, particularly with French yachtsmen. Given HTL's previous encounter with the French company TAG, it was understandable that there was an aversion to dealings with the French.

Solaris had sold one boat to Prince Ranier of Monaco as a wedding gift to his daughter, Princess Caroline, but still owed about £30,000 on the purchase. The receivable had been part of the asset package taken over by Hovermarine. Zebedee rang the

The Solaris 42′ catamaran

Prince and was eventually connected to his personal secretary. He explained the Prince's position was that the boat had not met specifications; that among other things the cushions in the main salon were soiled. Bill's response was to give the Prince seven days to pay or else the boat would be repossessed. He said he was experienced in such matters, and suggested that they review the French newspaper accounts of the TAG piracy incident for confirmation. The outstanding balance was promptly remitted.

There was another "interesting" French Solaris customer, Jean Yves Terlain, a well known long distance yachtsman. He had ordered a special 70' Solaris to sail in that year's single-handed transatlantic yacht race. He wanted it painted jet black and a Citroen car body installed as a wheelhouse to highlight his sponsors.

He insisted on a rather curious H mast rig. Two masts, stepped side by side with a cross brace, like a pair of rugby goal-posts. These were so tall that our people were worried the vessel wouldn't pass beneath the Itchen Bridge, even at spring low tide. Solaris were not on schedule for this build and with the race start not far away, Mr. Terlain was in an absolute passion for us to regain lost time. He pressed Mike Richards and Eaon Furnell daily for progress and, as was so often the case, they pulled the rabbit out of the hat and Mr. Terlain paid and departed for France just in time. He made it under the Itchen Bridge by a foot or two, with our people stationed anxiously on the apex to watch, and sailed away into history.

Hovermarine had also acquired all the Solaris inventories, amongst which were a partially built boat and virtually all the parts needed to complete the vessel, notably including its costly Mercedes propulsion engines. Along with Eaon Furnell, Bill decided to use the build completion as a "labor sink" for otherwise temporarily idled workers and then make it his personal yacht. When finished, he called a board of directors' meeting onboard. Practically as soon as they pulled away from the Hovermarine quay, Eaon became seasick, and no further board meetings were held at sea.

One Friday evening as he was about to leave, Bernie Magdovitz came to Bill. Bill had hired Bernie as Hovcorp's accounting manager, and transferred him to the UK in1976, naming him HTL's Financial Director.

Bernie said he had a Frenchman in his office who wanted to buy the personal yacht. Absolutely not, said Zebedee. Bernie replied, "But boss, he has cash...cash."

He had come across the Channel with a valise containing one

Former Supermarine Solaris plant, renamed Plant 2

million French Francs, and having smuggled it over, he was not about to carry it back to France. A deal was struck and the customer left the money as security.

Bernie proudly soon returned with the valise, but demurred on putting it in the company safe, saying he could open it in seconds with a can opener. Bill took the money home for the weekend, stacked the bills on his sitting room mantle, and detailed the family Olde English Sheep Dog ("Brigitte") to guard duty.

HOVERMARINE

CHAPTER ELEVEN

NON-FERRY APPLICATIONS

SHELL MARAVEN – VENEZUELA

IN EARLY 1978, BILL ZEBEDEE and Eaon Furnell visited Rotterdam as part of the contracting process with the Port Authority. As they had been invited to make a presentation at Royal Dutch Shell in the neighboring Hague, they had hired a car to get around. On concluding their meetings with the Port people, they headed to "Den Hague." They had an address for the Shell meeting.

Zebedee recalls, "I expected as we drove into the city that Shell would have a giant skyscraper with its logo emblazoned, and be readily visible. We soon discovered that The Hague was full of such buildings! We were hopelessly lost, and as the time of our appointment was fast approaching, Eaon managed to flag down a local taxi, and the driver agreed to lead us to the address. I had previously worked for the then world's largest corporation, General Motors, but I was unprepared for the enormity of the RDS presence in Holland.

"We made our meeting with only seconds to spare. Our hosts found it hilarious when we described our adventure in finding the place; I'm sure it was not the first time they had heard such stories. The meeting went quite well. When we returned to Woolston, we provided some follow-up information and then heard...nothing."

Some three months later, Eaon took a call from a chap who identified himself as a RDS contracting officer. He said he was flying to London the following morning and wanted to meet as soon as he could get to Southampton. The meeting began with brief pleasantries (the Dutch, we had learned, were not given to small talk), and then to our amazement he presented us with the RDS standard form marine contract, for the purchase of three craft and spare parts. He said there were three (and only three!) provisions in the contract that were negotiable. It was left to us to find them, and he noted that he needed to leave by mid-afternoon.

Bill recalls, "By sheer luck, our company solicitor, Phillip Ely, was in his office in Southampton, and he came over straight away to review the contract. We worked through lunch, and by 1330 we reconvened. Phillip had absolutely nailed the three soft spots! An hour later, we had a signed contract, and our newest best friend was on his way back home!"

From this encounter, Zebedee drew two conclusions. First, the Dutch were becoming his favorite people to deal with; smart, no nonsense, good sense of humor and straightforward. Second, the company needed its own in-house solicitor.

He was especially thankful to be dealing with RDS. Two years earlier, Venezuela had nationalized its domestic oil industry, and Maraven had become a contractor to the newly formed Petroleos de Venezuela S.A. (PDVSA), which was fast becoming a nightmare of bureaucracy and corruption. Maraven in turn had contracted with RDS, thus providing a double layer of separation from PDVSA.

The Maraven crewboat operation was an immediate success. Lake Maracaibo was an excellent operating environment for HM2s, and the Shell personnel were thoroughly professional. As the craft were being delivered, Hovermarine sent Peter White to Maracaibo to lead the training effort, and he summarizes his experience:

Shell Maraven craft on Lake Maracaibo, Venezuela (circa 1980)

"The craft was ideal for its role. Computer printouts were issued to the craft crew each morning that comprised of a list and order of oil rigs that had to be visited. The craft would then follow the prescribed route, picking up and dropping off crews at their allocated work stations. Berthing at all the different platforms was made with a bow on approach. Once the craft was in contact with the rig, with the engines slow ahead, the air cushion could be raised or lowered to match the craft height to that of the rig. The work crew could then pass safely over the bow between the conveniently placed hand rails, and whilst still under the direct observation of the Captain.

"One of the most useful things I was able to achieve working with Maraven was to list their inventory of Hovermarine spare parts and to set up a maximum and minimum stock holding for each part. The materials and purchasing departments would then automatically reorder as stocks were depleted. They continued to purchase parts for the next fifteen years."

The Hovermarine SES has revolutionised the method of crew-transfer from boat to oil rig. The craft's unique features of roll stability and station-keeping, together with its special bow-docking technique enabled crews to be transferred both quickly and safely

SHELL SINGAPORE

Hovermarine's working relationship with Royal Dutch Shell steadily strengthened, and by 1978, Shell was beginning to show interest in a crewboat service for its refinery in Singapore. Once more, the Gifford family moved.

Graham again picks up the narrative: "Most of my discussions with Shell were with the Marine Manager. He was a solid and very competent mariner who relaxed in super surroundings at his home on Bukom or at the Shell Club in the evenings! I believe he liaised with his London counterpart, but the decision to proceed was no doubt locally driven. In the event, it was a joy to deal with a customer prospect that had seemingly unlimited resources, who understood marine operations and the importance of keeping a full stock of spare parts to support an operation!

"A year later, just as I was transferring back to the UK, the decision was made to proceed with the purchase of five HM218s. From the start, it was a super route for HM2–Pasir Panjang (near the Tiger Balm Gardens) to Shell's Bukom Island Refinery and HQ—calm water, short distance, good payloads, frequent service and well run. I would put this operation amongst the very best we had for the HM2s."

GRAY MACKENZIE, BAHRAIN

Proving that word travels quickly in the oil patch, in 1979 HTL was contacted by Gray MacKenzie, then a major oilfield services company, headquartered in London. They provided a wide array of services to Saudi-based Aramco, the world's largest petroleum producer.

GrayMac rejected a 218 ferry configuration, primarily because they wanted to carry cargo as well as passengers, and the 218 was too small. However, a newly designed HM221 was on the drawing boards. They purchased the prototype, basing it in Bahrain as a demonstration platform.

The 221 was ten feet longer than the 218. The hull had been designed for the Tacoma fire boats, and Hovermarine engineers had redesigned the aft compartments to "sink" the engines profile down to the main deck, covering the engines with flat hatches. This left an expanse of rear deck suitable for cargo.

After a promising start, the project would prove to be a disappointment. Most important, the consortium of major oil companies that owned and operated Aramco were forced to turn the company over to Saudi Arabia, and many of the vendors, including GrayMac, thereafter abandoned their Arabian operations. Also, the HM221 was never fully optimized for rigorous oilfield service, including slamming of the hull against the oil rigs during crew transfers. Finally, even with its cargo

HM221 453 *"Grayspear"* was the first 21 meter HM2 delivered

deck, many rig components and spare parts were simply too heavy for the weight-sensitive HM2.

THE PORT OF ROTTERDAM

In 1976, representatives of the Port of Rotterdam approached HTL with a concept for a multi-mission port patrol and traffic management vessel. Still firmly planted in ferryboat thinking, the company was lukewarm to the POR idea. Fortunately Nigel Gee, by then Hovermarine's chief naval architect, had other ideas. Working with the customer through a series of design iterations, they came to an agreed design from which Nigel had a model made for approval by the POR board. Rotterdam wanted to purchase four craft.

The company and particularly Bill Zebedee were evolving from their ferryboat mentality, and towards a business model

Two of the HM218s patrolling the Rotterdam harbor

of custom design, utilizing the HM2 and future sidewall designs as marine platforms. Any application that could benefit from greater speed became a customer prospect. For example, the more quickly a fireboat could get to a fire, the more easily the fire could be brought under control and extinguished.

Contract terms were agreed, and in mid-1977 Hovermarine went to work on detailed design and construction. The specifications were complex. The craft had multiple marine radios to communicate with shipping traffic, a fire fighting monitor on top of the wheelhouse, and various emergency rescue equipment.

Originally, the craft were to be equipped with a boom-mounted CCTV camera to enable the crew to peer over the main decks of very large ocean-going vessels. During trials, this feature would prove problematic. CCTV cameras were then still quite heavy, and when the booms were extended to their full

50 foot height, their base was still an HM2 in typical turbulent harbor sea conditions. The poles flexed as if they were fly fishing rods that had hooked a whale!

The first craft, *Havendienst 10* (449), was presented at a commissioning ceremony in 1978 on the Hazel Wharf pier, attended by executives of the Port.

Bill Zebedee (left) making remarks at the Rotterdam ceremony. Standing alongside is the Managing Director of the Port and his wife, with Port officers in the background.

PORT OF TACOMA FIREBOATS

The city of Tacoma, Washington, lies some 7,000 miles east of Southampton, and seemed a most unlikely place for a small fast ferry company from the South of England to appear.

Hovermarine's involvement came about through a Marine Consultant called Owen Douglas. He lived in the Tacoma area and was contracted by the Tacoma Fire Department to design a fire boat that would set a new standard for state-of-the-art. There was more than a tinge of competition involved with Tacoma's neighboring "big sister" city of Seattle, which had just purchased a new USA built Fireboat.

Owen Douglas came up with a design around the Hovermarine platform, and specifications that no other conventional vessel could match. It should be noted that at the time there were only thirty-nine dedicated fireboats in the whole of the US. Most harbor authorities were satisfied with a fire pump and monitors mounted on ten knot tug boats.

The City of Tacoma raised a bond of $750,000 to cover the cost of two boats. The measure passed a public vote with the promise of a reduction in fire insurance premiums for all waterfront properties located in Southern Puget Sound.

From the start it was apparent that the bond proceeds would be woefully short of the costs for the two boats. Nonetheless, Bill Zebedee was intrigued. If the available money could at least cover the direct cost of building the craft, it could set a new worldwide standard for fireboats, with Hovermarine in a preeminent position. Yes, Hovermarine would have to absorb the design costs, but Bill reasoned that they could be amortized over future sales.

Eating the cost overruns would turn out to be quite the meal! Early on, it was clear that the City's performance demands could not fit into a sixty-foot HM218 platform, and so the seventy-foot HM221 was born. Erling Mork, the City Manager, and Tony Mitchell, Fire Chief, insisted on a clear aft deck, necessitating a redesign so the propulsion engines could be placed lower in the hull and covered by flush hatches.

They also specified six fire monitors, two below the bow, two on the fore deck, one on the high lift access crane and ladder. The sixth, a large bore nozzle aft of the wheelhouse had to take the full flow of all three fire pumps, 7,500 gallons/minute, and throw an arc of water that could land up to 400 feet away, or knock down a brick wall at a distance of 165 feet. All the firemain system valves were electro-hydraulically operated from joysticks on the fire officer's panel in the wheelhouse. During final trials in Southampton and the early days in Tacoma Peter White was one of only two people that knew how to operate the full fire system. At full flow, a wrong setting could have sunk the boat in a matter of seconds!

But in terms of cost, the real "show stopper" would come when the design was nearly complete. Ted Tattersall announced that the craft was too heavy and would not be able to meet its thirty-knot speed specification unless the firemain was made of titanium instead of stainless steel. Titanium is roughly twenty thousand times more costly than steel!

This move alone cost hundreds of thousands of dollars and made the boats so expensive as to prohibit future sales. Zebedee seriously was thinking of abandoning the project, but with the appearance of Vosper, the project proceeded.

In the event, the first two 221 hulls were built in 1979, and outfitting commenced following the Vosper takeover in 1980, one for Gray MacKenzie and the other to be the first Tacoma craft, named *Defiance*. Both would be delivered in 1982, with the second Tacoma fireboat, called *Commencement* following in 1983.

Though a financial disaster for Vosper and Hovermarine, the Tacoma boats were an unqualified technical success. Over the following decade, the Fire Department would learn that a single high speed boat was sufficient, and in 1995 *Defiance* was withdrawn from service. Nigel Gee and Associates, by then a world

HM221 465 "*Defiance*" passing the Tacoma Dome sports arena

renowned naval design firm, took a contract to overhaul *Commencement*. She remains the flagship of the Tacoma fireboat fleet to this day.

Furthermore, the hope for future sales was seemingly justified when, in 1986, Vosper Hovermarine licensed the Tacoma design to Textron Marine & Land Services of New Orleans, an American shipbuilding subsidiary of Textron Inc. Another Textron subsidiary had designed and built the Landing Craft Air Cushion (LCAC) hovercraft operated by the U.S. Navy.

Commencement after refit. Note that base color was changed to international orange

At the Tacoma inauguration ceremony. *L to R*: Chief Tony Mitchell, City Manager Erling Mork, Port of Rotterdam Engineer Koos Wernsing, Eaon Furnell, Tacoma Deputy Mayor Harold Moss, Robert Ducane, and Bill Zebedee

Textron would sell two copies of the Tacoma boat to the New York City Fire Department in 1989. At the time, they were hailed as the harbor firefighters of the future.

Meantime, Hovermarine had gone bankrupt, and so a group of ex-employees formed a group to construct the hulls in a leased section of the old Solaris plant and ship them to New Orleans for outfitting. In 1992 during sea trials, the union representing the NYCFD workers demanded the craft carry a permanent crew of twelve. The city refused and broke the contract with Textron. Both craft were left tied up at a pier nearby the Statue of Liberty.

In 1997, Peter White was asked by Textron to survey the boats. He found them in remarkably good shape; they were, after all, hardly used. They remain today at that location, abandoned.

HOVERMARINE

CHAPTER TWELVE

ENTER VOSPER

BY LATE 1978 THE FLOOR space problem had been solved with the Solaris acquisition, but financial problems were still a major concern. Bill Zebedee was feeling the full burden of the company's precarious condition, and takes up the narrative:

"Our sales growth was almost overwhelming. The order backlog was approaching £50 million. We had nearly 700 employees; weekly payroll demands were massive. We had developed concepts such as contractual stage payments to maximize cash flow, but growth was still devouring cash faster than we could bring it in the door. Neither Lloyds Bank nor my old friend Tom Herlihy at Chase Manhattan Bank was interested in helping. Hovcorp shares were trading below $3.00 in the U.S. market, so there was no appetite for another share offering. I had the feeling that I was surrounded by a team of hundreds of people doing their best to contribute to the company's success while I was not doing my job.

"In December, a few days from the Company's two-week holiday shutdown, I received a call from Sir John Rix, asking if he might pay me a visit. I had met John (before he was knighted) in 1973. He was then Managing Director of Vosper Thornycroft, the British warship builder located on the Itchen just down from Hazel Wharf. Then facing eviction by Baring Brothers, I had been looking for manufacturing space. VT had nothing available, but our meeting had been cordial. Of course, I now agreed to see him.

"The next day Sir John came to my office. After pleasantries, he came to the point of his visit, saying that they had been watching our progress with keen interest, and wondered if we might be interested in selling the company or taking on a partner.

"Absolutely not, I replied, adding that I was thoroughly enjoying the excitement and challenge of running such a growing enterprise. He asked if he might provide a proposal in writing. I told him he could do as he liked, but added my family and I were about to leave for a skiing holiday in Switzerland.

"The next day, his driver dropped off a bulky sealed envelope. I left in unopened on my desk and departed for the Swiss Alps.

"Truly my first reaction had been an honest feeling; I had zero interest in selling. However, skiing has a way of focusing one's mind. For me, the focus was usually terror—I was not all that good on skis! However, in the evenings, sitting in front of a roaring fire with a glass of good whiskey, I started thinking *What if this were another bolt from Heaven, ala Solaris?* It was certainly an alternative I had not contemplated, but I began seeing it as my fiduciary duty to shareholders, creditors, employees and customers to at least give it due consideration.

"Shortly after I returned from holiday, Sir John rang to say he was wondering what I thought. 'About what?' I asked (perhaps a bit too coy)? I must have annoyed him, but he replied, 'Our proposal of course.' I told him I had been so busy I had not even opened the envelope, but promised I would get to it in the next few days.

"Over the next three moths talks continued, I kept running away from Rix, but only fast enough to let him keep up. Somewhere in the early spring we agreed on terms, but I knew this would mark only the starting point of negotiations to come. I had learned that Sir David Brown, a noted British industrialist, was the controlling shareholder of Vosper, so I also knew the deal was going nowhere until he approved."

In the spring of 1979, Hovermarine was visited by The Man

himself, seventy-five-year-old Sir David Brown. As a man of notable wealth and a tax exile living in Monaco, he could not afford to die on English soil, so he flew in by private aircraft to the Southampton airport, accompanied by his personal physician.

Bill recounts, "The Vosper board members turned up in our carpark, shoes polished and well ahead of Sir David's expected arrival time. In pulled an enormous Rolls Royce. The driver opened the back door and he emerged. I was struck by his diminutive stature; he was no more than five and a half feet tall. After introductions, I said we thought an HM2 demonstration should be the first order of business as the tides were favorable. Sir David asked if Paula might come along. I had no clue as to Paula. Sir John shrugged and Sir David motioned to the driver to open the car door.

"Out came a very attractive leg, followed by the second, both feet in stiletto heels. As Paula emerged, it was obvious to all that her beauty did not stop with her legs. She had to be some six feet tall and striking in those high heals! I judged she could be no more than thirty years old. Nothing quite like her had ever before appeared at Hovermarine!

"We all boarded the HM2. Our skipper was Senior Captain Bill Thwaites. When Paula asked to go to the pilot house, poor Bill was so distracted he nearly collided with a bridge support column as we exited the River Itchen.

"On returning, the party entered the Hazel Wharf plant and climbed the long flight of stairs to the balcony overlooking the plant floor. I'll never know how Paula, in her high heels, made it up those steps. All sounds of work ceased, and some 200 pairs of eyes firmly fixed on a single target.

"Sir David observed, 'Your blokes don't seem to be working very hard.' Suppressing a laugh, I mumbled something about them rarely seeing such distinguished visitors."

It was soon apparent Sir David had approved, and negotiations picked up pace. Given access to Hovermarine's books,

Vosper found reasons to reduce the agreed price. Notable was the projected loss on the Tacoma fireboat contract; as Bill would later say, "Not even a goat could have missed that!"

After nearly a year of negotiations, the showdown came on New Year's Eve 1979, in the London offices of the Vosper solicitors. The scene was almost comical. Sir John Rix was in formal wear; no doubt running late for a party with Lady Rix, who must have been similarly attired and waiting in a car at the curb. Rix was attempting some last minute maneuvers, and Zebedee finally said, "Enough! Sign the deal on the table or else tomorrow morning [New Year's Day] Hovermarine will no longer be for sale." Rix signed, and Vosper took control on January 1, 1980, promptly renaming the company Vosper Hovermarine Limited.

Along the way, Bill had done some of his own due diligence on Vosper. He learned that Vosper Thornycroft had, along with the entire UK shipbuilding industry, been nationalized in 1977. When the smoke had cleared the remains, named Vosper PLC, consisted of a small ship repair facility in Singapore and a massive lawsuit against the British government.

The Aircraft and Shipbuilding Industries Act 1977 had set a statutory price formula for the nationalization takeovers based on each company's average share price for a six month period ended in February 1974. Three years later when the Act was finally passed by Parliament, Vosper was awarded £10 million under the legislation, despite then having £12 million in the bank and showing substantial annual profits. In the true British sense of fair play, the Government agreed to pay appellants' legal expenses if they chose to litigate, but a little-noticed provision (Section 42) of the Act limited the courts to hear only appeals over valuation, but not challenges to the fairness of the statutory formula. Of the eighteen shipbuilders nationalized, Vosper and two others appealed.

At the time of the Hovermarine takeover, it was widely expected that the courts would eventually award Vosper some £80 million. No one exuded more confidence than Sir John Rix, who was positively indignant that the Labour government had treated his company so unfairly. Banks were lined up to shower the company with loans and he happily accepted the borrowings.

In mid-1980, the shipbuilders lost their appeals in the British courts but this did little to dampen enthusiasm. They filed actions with the European Court of Human Rights. These proceedings would drag on for the next six years.

HOVERMARINE

PART THREE

1980 – 1986

The Vosper Years

HOVERMARINE

CHAPTER THIRTEEN

1980–1983: THE BEGINNING OF THE END

THE NEW YEAR BEGAN WITH Bill Zebedee moving to offices in Vosper House in Fareham and becoming Vice Chairman of the newly named Vosper Hovermarine, with Sir John Rix taking over as Chairman. Mike Richards remained as the company's Managing Director. Operations were initially little affected.

Fareham was much different. Bill recounts: "I was accustomed to having a pint-and-a-pie lunch with the lads at Hovermarine. Not so at Vosper House, where every day the directors gathered in the boardroom for drinks, wine and at least a three-course luncheon, nearly always presided over by Sir John. Afternoons were mainly occupied (at least in my case) with sleeping off the effects of the alcohol before attempting to drive home. I hated it.

"However, it was of no real consequence. With Mike in charge, little changed at Hazel Wharf. I had agreed to remain for a year, primarily because of my relationship with Edmond Lau and my contacts in Japan at Hovermarine Pacific. My course was set; I was on my way out.

"The Vosper board were generally a decent but weak lot. Ken Ford, finance director, was a milquetoast, frightened to death of Rix. Peter Shepherd, sales director, was something of a blowhard. The dangerous one was Robert Ducane; he had no portfolio.

"I had met Robert during a visit to Singapore in 1979; he was then MD of Vosper Singapore. I believe he was a younger brother of Peter Ducane, the near-legendary designer of the VT warships. I never met Peter, by then deceased, but Robert certainly could not have been cut from the same cloth. I found him a classic ne'er-do-well, stuffy and totally incompetent. When I returned to the UK, Sir John asked how I had gotten on with Robert. Shortly thereafter, he replaced Robert but kept him on the board. Later, I would learn that Sir David was Robert's protector.

"Mike Richards was now free of money concerns and largely left alone by the Vosper crowd, save perhaps for Rix's cadre of underutilized and inexperienced engineers who were keen to make a banquet of Hovermarine's technical challenges.

"One day in early summer, I attended the usual directors' luncheon at Vosper House. Robert Ducane was just back from a lengthy visit with David Brown in Monaco and attempting to regale us with stories of his exploits. My first reaction was boredom, but I began to detect an underlying message. After lunch, Sir John asked that I come to his office.

"He started by saying that he was not altogether happy with Mike's performance, and he thought 'we' should consider a change. He said he had already asked Mike to come over and join us a bit later. Suddenly the picture was clear. I told John that 'we' were not going to fire Mike; if he was intent on doing it he must do it himself. I also told him that if he planned on Robert as the replacement, I was dead set against it. Shortly thereafter, Ducane was announced as the new MD of Vosper Hovermarine. At that point, I mentally 'checked out' of Vosper."

Mike Richards was gone. Bill Zebedee was virtually gone. Graham Gifford was just back from Singapore and clashing with Peter Shepherd about selling in the commercial market. Peter

White, as usual, was abroad, doing his best to keep customers happy. Of all the authors of this manuscript, only Rod Wilkins and Eaon Furnell were left in the Boardroom.

Rod picks up the narrative: "1980 dawned with the Company under new ownership. This Vosper was not the naval shipbuilder whose huge yard was next to ours in Woolston. That was a nationalized firm. This was the post nationalization rump of the original, with no UK building capability, although some in Singapore. Their people were all experts in naval vessel design and build, far removed from our markets and clients.

"The Vosper team were old shipbuilding hands. Naval shipbuilders all, they had become frustrated by the lack of activity forced on them by the nationalization of their naval construction yard. They were dying to get their hands on our organization. Their view on life was conditioned by their experiences in government construction. Get a complex specification agreed, with every part detailed however big or small. Establish a cost for everything, then add a generous profit margin, and the total of all that equaled the buyer's price. Go to work and build! What the commercial market might stand for price and delivery times was a secondary and minor consideration. Better to hold to a substantial profit margin and make no sale than price to the market.

"Their leadership was all a generation older than Bill's team. Set in their ways and convinced of their superiority, they had luxury offices inland a few miles away from Hazel Wharf with a splendid director's dining room where they met daily to lunch over gin, sherry and a good robust red wine.

"We had been a pint of beer and a pie in the pub team. Regular meetings were few; formality absent. When we needed to get together we did so ad hoc. Now we needed an appointment to meet our Vosper colleagues.

"I don't recall ever seeing an organization chart during my time at Hovermarine. Vosper had theirs down to a 'T.' Our budget for the few company cars we owned was governed by the price of the car. Vosper had a complex algorithm established to ensure no one had a 'better' car than they were entitled to.

"The coming culture clash was easy to anticipate. They knew their business, but not ours. Notwithstanding, they were determined to impose their way. The air in our bubble began to leak, slowly at first, but ever faster after Mike Richards was replaced by Robert Ducane, a cold hearted man if I ever saw one. Formality, structure and rigidity dampened the 'can-do' spirit and agility of the firm. All this was at a time when England had seemed to be in gradual and painful decline. It was Pre-Thatcher.

"Ducane had no prior experience on directing commercial shipbuilding. Cold, distant, imperious, he knew better than us all; sought no counsel, brooked no opposition. Ruling by threats, he never established a following at Hovermarine and was near universally feared rather than respected. Not that he would have cared. He, like the rest of the Vosper crew, were certain of success in their lawsuit in the European Court of Human Rights, and expected a rain of capital to come from that. Their business decisions were underpinned by that assumption. They bet the store on it and overcommitted the company financially as a result."

Graham Gifford: "You may recall I got up at one company meeting at the Botley Country Hotel and told Sir John Rix, Peter Shepherd and the others assembled that I thought the present prices and way of business would lead to disaster. I might as well have been talking to the wall."

Eaon Furnell remained as Manufacturing Director of VHL, and recounts the following: "One afternoon Mike Richards returned from a meeting at Vosper House. He called me to his office and told me he had just been sacked. He said he suspected that Robert Ducane would be his replacement. The following morning, Mike's prediction became fact.

"I was soon summoned to meet with our new Managing Director. One of the first things he said to me was that I must address him as 'Mister Ducane.' I replied, 'That's OK; you can call me Mister Furnell.' It was to be all downhill from there!

"He would ring me and say he was coming over to visit the men on the lower deck. I would ask who he meant.

"He and I were invited to the opening ceremony of the Tacoma fire boats by Erling Mork, the City Manager. His secretary told me she had booked our flights and that he was in first class and I was in business. When I questioned this he said all main board directors travel in first.

"Erling asked me to stay an extra couple of days after Ducane had left. I officially signed the craft over to the City, and Erling then took me back to his house for drinks, followed by dinner with his wife and daughter. It was a celebration of the end of a few enjoyable years. When I got back Ducane was not at all happy to have been ignored.

"There are many other stories I could tell of that period, but they all add up to the utter contempt I developed for this man and what he was doing to the Company I loved."

It's official—the city owns new fireboat

By BRUCE JOHNSON

The City of Tacoma's new hovercraft fireboat officially belongs to the city now, in the wake of a signing-of-documents ceremony yesterday in the conference room of City Manager Erling O. Mork.

Ownership of the 70-foot vessel was transferred to the city from British shipbuilder Vosper Hovermarine Ltd. following two weeks of successful city-acceptance sea trials.

The air-cushion craft, first of its kind in the world, performed flawlessly during its 37 hours of operation since the fiberglass boat arrived here less than a month ago, said Owen Douglas, the city's fireboat construction consultant.

The diesel-powered, propeller-driven boat passed with flying colors such city performance specifications as zipping across the water at 30 knots with minimal wake and pumping at least 5,500 gallons per minute of water from its monitors, he said.

Yesterday's acceptance of the vessel, which involved a final city payment of $152,000 to Vosper Hovermarine, is contingent on the craft's fulfilling three more contract performance specifications, Douglas said.

"But the craft will do what it's supposed to do," he said. "I have no doubt about it."

Douglas said those figures will be gathered during city fireboat crew training, which begins Monday, and a federal government-funded hovercraft fireboat missions study due to get under way in about six weeks.

Signing the "protocol of delivery and acceptance" papers for the city were Mork, Fire Chief Tony Mitchell and John Maddock, research and development administrator for the Tacoma Fire Department.

Signing on behalf of the boat's builder was Eaon Furnell, manufacturing director for Southampton-based Vosper Hovermarine.

Staff photo by BRUCE KELLMAN

Eaon Furnell, left, Erling Mork and Tony Mitchell

From the *Tacoma News Tribune* reporting on the transfer of ownership of *Defiance* and *Commencement* to the city

HOVERMARINE

CHAPTER FOURTEEN

AWARDS

WE GAVE SOME THOUGHT TO subtitling this chapter "Too Little, Too Late," but Hovermarine finally received recognition for its accomplishments; albeit after it came under Vosper control.

In April 1985 the Company received the Design Council Award for its "HM200 and HM500 Series of Hovercraft," presented to Ted Tattersall by HRH The Duke of Edinburgh at the Montague Estate on the Beaulieu River in the New Forest.

A year later, MD Eaon Furnell was invited to Buckingham Palace to receive The Queen's Award for Export Achievement. These were proud occasions for the many men and women of Hovermarine who worked so hard for the Company's success.

Bill Zebedee recalls having dinner one evening with Sir John when the subject of awards (the lack thereof) came up. Sir John remarked that he was not sure that we would want the Queen's Award as it was known as the "plastic tombstone."

How prophetic....

ELIZABETH THE SECOND,

by the Grace of God of the United Kingdom of Great Britain and Northern Ireland and of Our other Realms and Territories Queen Defender of the Faith, to

VOSPER HOVERMARINE LTD

Greeting!

We being cognisant of the outstanding achievement of the said body as manifested in the furtherance and increase of the Export Trade of Our United Kingdom of Great Britain and Northern Ireland, Our Channel Islands and Our Island of Man and being desirous of showing Our Royal Favour do hereby confer upon it

THE QUEEN'S AWARD FOR EXPORT ACHIEVEMENT

for a period of five years from the twenty-first day of April 1984 until the twentieth day of April 1989 and do hereby give permission for the authorised flag of the said Award to be flown during that time by the said body and for the device thereof to be displayed in the manner authorised by Our Warrant of the fifth day of April 1976.

And We do further hereby authorise the said body during the five years of the currency of this Our Award further to use and display in like manner the flags and devices of any current former Awards by it received as prescribed in the eighth Clause of Our said Warrant.

Given at Our Court at St. James's under Our Royal Sign Manual this twenty-first day of April in the year of Our Lord 1984 in the thirty-third year of Our Reign.

By the Sovereign's Command.

The Design Award and proceedings, with HRH Prince Phillip (*center*) preparing to inspect an HM2

CHAPTER FIFTEEN

1983–1986: THE END OF THE END

EAON FURNELL CONTINUES: "IN OCTOBER 1983, I was asked to go and see Rix at his Fareham Office. I was shocked and surprised when he asked me to become VHL Managing Director. Aside from sheer joy of the prospect of seeing the last of Ducane, I said I wasn't sure I had the right sort of background to do the job, that my frontline business, contracts experience etc were not great. He said he was aware of that, and that he and Ken Ford, and particularly Denis Kemp, would support me. I knew that my wish to win was equal to or greater than others so I said yes.

"I had just plunged from the frying pan right into the fire! We were building out our last few orders for HM2s and completing the last HM5 for Hong Kong. The cost-plus mindset had strangled our sales effort, and the lack of attention to innovation or diversification had left us with nowhere to go. We had an enormous overhead, including a year-round suite at London's Dorchester Hotel for Sir David and Ducane. I turned to the only man I thought could help me.

"Denis Kemp was very close friend to Rix. He had worked for many years at Vosper Thornycroft and retired as Director of Business. He was the only real English Gentleman I ever mixed

(*L to R*): Sir John Rix; Eaon Furnell; and Ken Ford, Vosper Financial Director

with. He was very well spoken. I never heard him swear or talk badly about anyone. Denis and I, with input from Nigel Gee, took a hard look at the high speed catamaran market. Nigel was very keen and convincing with some good ideas.

"Denis was an independent consultant on a part time contract, and was very helpful and supportive of me, especially in my efforts to diversify. We became good friends and met up from time to time after I retired until he died."

Another friend was Bill Zebedee, back in America for three years when Eaon became Managing Director. Bill had severed all ties to Vosper and was Chairman of a company called Dollar Corporation. Dollar had a subsidiary, Dollar Energy Systems. When Eaon contacted him to tell of his promotion and his desire to diversify, Bill had an idea to help both companies.

Dollar Energy Systems had taken over an eighty-unit windfarm in Tehachapi, California. The project was a disaster. The

In Hong Kong with (*R to L*) Nigel Gee, Eaon Furnell, PRC official, and Denis Kemp

windmills were driven by blades made of fiberglass, but they had proven unable to stand up to the high winds that frequented Tehachapi Pass.

Aided by a multi-million dollar insurance settlement, Dollar needed a redesign and new blades, and the need was urgent if the company was to preserve its tax benefits.

Bill reasoned that Hovermarine was among the best in the world at fiberglass construction, and knew that, if anyone could meet his urgent schedule, it was Eaon and his people. Bill dispatched Steve Brown, Dollar's head of windfarm systems, to England. Steve contacted a company called Gifford Technology, located in the New Forest area near Southampton. Gifford produced a new design and a wooden plug, from which VHL constructed moulds.

Soon, blades nineteen-feet long were pouring from the Hazel Wharf factory, loaded straight onto British Airways 747 cargo planes and flown to Los Angeles. As they arrived on site, they

Dollar Energy Systems windfarm with new blades from Hovermarine

were immediately mounted and started producing electricity. In all, VHL produced 240 blades, on time and within budget.

Thereafter Eaon negotiated a £1,000,000 contract with Howden Engineering of Glasgow to produce blades to their specifications. This business might well have saved Hovermarine, as fiberglass blades became the worldwide standard for wind turbines, and grew dramatically in size, complexity, price and unit volume. Regrettably, the opportunity would be overtaken by events.

Eaon continues: "Sir John had told me our best chance of survival was to win the legal case for compensation being brought against government, and my job was to get us there.

"I knew from my predecessors that the chief executive had to be involved in sales. Bill Zebedee and Mike Richards had built the order book. Ducane and, to an extent, John Rix had proven the opposite. So I visited San Francisco and other places I can't even remember. One promising trip was to Dubai to promote service to Abu Dhabi. I think we could have eventually done that deal, but we were running out of time. By the way, that's me on the left, doing my best 007 impersonation.

"Sometime after that Sir John introduced me to Roy Watts

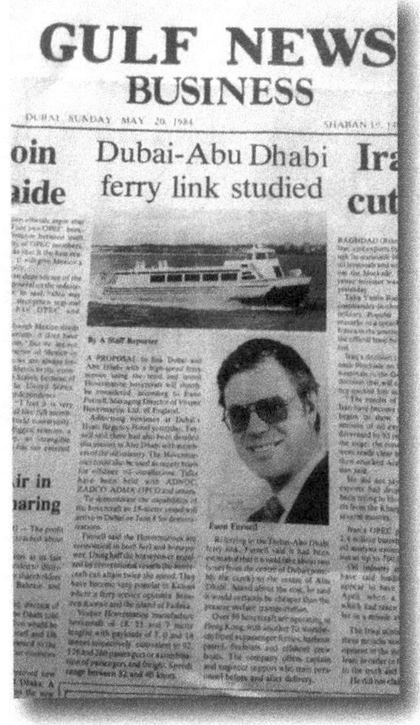
GULF NEWS
BUSINESS

Dubai-Abu Dhabi ferry link studied

who was to take over as chairman as he was retiring. I was very disappointed in Rix. As I saw it he was making sure he would not be the front man if the company collapsed, and I wondered if he knew the court case was about to fail.

"Roy Watts was still the Chairman of Thames Water at that time. I got on really well with him. He rarely came to VHL and would regularly call me up to his plush offices in Smiths Square, next door to Conservative headquarters in London. It was a bit of a bore but the lunches were good. On occasion he would ask Ken Ford to join us, but it became clear that they had quite opposing views when it came to finances and the way forward as things were getting tight.

"Some of the top guys started leaving. I had already laid off most of the original Vosper men, the last being Peter Shepherd. He had been in Indonesia for months constantly telling me he was about to sign a contract. I was losing any faith in what he said and decided to go and find out for myself. Whilst there I received a phone call telling me to catch the next flight home if I wanted to be in my office before the liquidators. I just made it.

"The liquidators allowed me to break the news to the company, so I got them all together and explained the situation. There were lots of comments but the overall feeling was one of sadness for an end that for me and many others had been the best days of our working lives."

* * * *

On Wednesday May 23, 1986, Eaon Furnell stepped into the Hazel Wharf factory and turned off the lights, as he had done

The Solaris plant, sold by the liquidators. Photo courtesy *Fast Ferry International*

for the best part of his twenty years with Hovermarine. "On this night," he recalls, "I had to walk away from the most exciting and rewarding time of my life. I cried all the way home."

* * * *

Editor's Note: Company histories are always filled with "what if" scenarios. What if we had not closed the HYF contract when we did? What if there had been no Solaris? The list goes on.

With the benefit of hindsight, the biggest question is What if we had turned down the Vosper deal? The reality was they had only borrowed money to offer Hovermarine, a ticking time bomb underlying the premise that the courts would grant them additional compensation. Of all the what ifs, this should have been the easiest to identify as false. The Enabling Act had allowed British courts no latitude to change the terms. The final appeal to the European Court of Human Rights was never more than a pipedream...one of its forty-seven judges was quoted as saying that nationalization was the only way to protect workers from the ravages of capitalism.

APPENDICES

HOVERMARINE

APPENDIX A: A PRIMER ON HOVERCRAFT

We judge that many of our readers will be knowledgeable on the subject of hovercraft. Many will be veterans of the industry, including those who remain of the some one thousand employees who were employed by Hovermarine. However, the last Hovermarine designed craft; indeed the last commercial hovercraft was produced more than thirty years ago. For those who may not be familiar with the technology we offer this short explanation.

ANY MARINE VESSEL IS SUBJECT to the basic rule of *displacement*. Simply put, if a ten-tonne boat is going to float, it must displace ten tonnes of water, and still have some reserve buoyancy to keep a portion of the vessel above the waterline. In order that the vessel move forward, it must have an energy source, typically some form of propulsion, capable of pushing ten tonnes of water out of the way in order to move forward by one boat length. Increasing the strength of the energy source allows the vessel to achieve greater speed, but it is still subject to the rule of *displacement*—it must push aside ten tonnes of water each time it moves forward one boat length.

All vessels are governed by the same rule. A ten-tonne hovercraft sitting stationary on its own air cushion is using an air bubble to create a "hole" of ten tonnes in the water. Now if one applies sufficient energy, the vessel can effectively outrun its hole and achieve what is known as surface effect. The objective is to have just enough energy to achieve this surface effect;

once accomplished the vessel is effectively flying, and since air is one-tenth the density of water, relatively high speeds can be achieved efficiently.

Sir Christopher and Lady Cockerell with Marian Richards at Hazel Wharf for the Port of Rotterdam celebration

From the start, the hovercraft fraternity was separated into two main camps. The true amphibian craft side was represented by Sir Christopher Cockerell, widely regarded as the father of the hovercraft. The air cushion was generated by one or more fans, and contained by a flexible, rubber-like skirt around the entire periphery of the craft, with propulsion provided by aircraft propellers.

An offshoot of the amphibian were the so-called sidewall hovercrafts, also known as surface effect ships. They used solid sidewalls, never emerging from the water, together with skirts fore and aft to contain the air. They were thus not amphibians, and so could be driven by conventional marine propellers.

Ted Tattersall (*R*) with HRH The Duke of Edinburgh (*L*) and Vosper's Sir John Rix

Leading the sidewall design effort was a young Cockerell protégé named Ted Tattersall. He was a true believer in sidewall technology, and in 1965 he and a small group of associates formed Hovermarine Ltd. Essentially the sidewall supporters traded off amphibious capability to achieve three important objectives. First, sidewall craft had far less air escape. The flexible skirts were simply inefficient at trapping air under pressure, and so considerably greater power was needed to generate and maintain the cushion of an amphibian. Second, amphibians were far more weight sensitive, which necessitated powering these craft with expensive gas turbine engines, far more costly to purchase and operate than the far heavier Diesel engines that were suitable for sidewall craft. Finally, it was widely acknowledged that sidewall designs would become more efficient as they were scaled up in size, whereas the opposite was true for amphibious designs.

Through most of its history, Hovermarine was crucially supported by Hovercraft Development Limited (HDL), a subsidiary of the National Research Development Council, a Crown Corporation whose charter was to safeguard and support British technology.

APPENDIX B: BRITISH GOVERNMENT AGENCIES THAT SUPPORTED HOVERMARINE

NATIONAL RESEARCH DEVELOPMENT CORPORATION (NRDC)

This Crown Corporation, now part of the British Technology Group, was established in 1948 to facilitate British-developed technology transfer from the public to the private sector. Through a subsidiary, Hovercraft Development Limited (HDL), it held the patents on air-cushion vessels, and in 1958 contracted for construction of the first commercial-size hovercraft. In the mid-1960s, HDL provided seed money for the then-nascent Hovermarine Ltd.

NRDC's implicit mission was to protect British technology from foreigners, and the takeover of Hovermarine by an American company in 1969 must have been anathema to the Corporation. HDL did agree to provide a license to the Americans, but there was no financial support for the ensuing six years. The 1976 closure of the Hovermarine Corporation (Hovcorp) offices and factory can be seen as a positive signal of commitment to Britain, and HDL thereafter provided substantial funding for the design and development of the HM5.

EXPORT CREDITS GUARANTEE DEPARTMENT (ECGD)

ECGD was formed in 1919 as a department of Her Majesty's Government to provide government financial support, direct financing, guarantees, insurance or interest rate support to foreign buyers of British products. This was a global first, and the program has since been copied in many other countries, not least the US Export- Import Bank. Still popularly known by its original name, it currently is called UK Export Finance (UKEF) and is a division of the Department for International Trade.

ECGD provides financial and political insurance for UK exports, making its own credit decisions and charging fees commensurate with the risk. With an ECGD policy, long term funding for exports can be readily provided by almost any international bank. Payment for more than half of Hovermarine's total exports were ECGD guaranteed.

Hovermarine vessels were built to Lloyds or Det Norske Veritas standards which provided the product quality assurance ECGD required. Many policies were straightforward, such as sales to the Hong Kong ferry company: the company had excellent credit and the Colony (in the 1970s) was not judged a political risk. Others such as Bolivia carried substantial commercial and political risk. In the event of default, Hovermarine was committed to assist ECGD in loan resolution and – if required – remarketing, but undertook no financial liability.

NRDC and ECGD were important contributors to Hovermarine's successes. Other countries offer similar government assistance, but most focus on very large corporations. Small or large, eligible British enterprises will be well advised to take advantage of the benefits offered by such agencies.

APPENDIX C:
BUILD AND ORIGINAL SALE HISTORY

No.	Build year	Type	Customer	Country
001	1968	216	British Rail Hovercraft	UK
002	1968	216	Hoverlink	UK
003	1968	216	Hoverspeed	Bahamas
004	1968	216	British Rail Hovercraft	UK
005	1968	216	International Hoverservices	UK
006	1968	216	Companhia de Navigacao Bahiana	Brazil
007	1968	216	British Rail Hovercraft	UK
008	1968	216	Hoverlink	UK
009	1969	216	East Pakistan Water Authority	Pakistan
010	1969	216	UK Government	UK
011	1969	216	Toryoung - Niagara Falls	USA
012	1969	216	International Hoverservices	UK
013	1969	216	Pertamina	Indoneaia
314	1972	216	City & Industrial Development	India
315	1972	216	Ministry of Public Works	Belgium
316	1972	216	Sociedade do Adoxe	Portugal
317	1972	216	De Bla Omnibusser	Norway
318	1973	216	Sociedade do Adoxe	Portugal
319	1973	216	Dolphin Ferries	Australia
320	1974	216	International Hoverservices	UK
321	1974	216	Servicos de Transportes da Baia	Brazil
322	1974	216	Servicos de Transportes da Baia	Brazil
323	1974	216	Servicos de Transportes da Baia	Brazil
324	1974	216	Hovermarine Titicaca	Bolivia
325	1974	216	Tourismo Margarita	Venezuela
326	1974	216	Hongkong & Yaumati Ferry Co. Ltd.	Hong Kong
327	1975	216	Hongkong & Yaumati Ferry Co. Ltd.	Hong Kong
328	1975	216	Hongkong & Yaumati Ferry Co. Ltd.	Hong Kong
329	1975	216	Hongkong & Yaumati Ferry Co. Ltd.	Hong Kong
330	1975	216	Tourismo Margarita	Venezuela
331	1975	216	Tourismo Margarita	Venezuela
332	1975	216	Bataan-Manila Fery Services	Philippines
333	1976	216	Hover d'Azur	France
334	1976	216	Hovermarine Pacific	Japan
435	1976	218	Hongkong & Yaumati Ferry Co. Ltd.	Hong Kong

HOVERMARINE

336	1976	216	Bataan-Manila Ferry Services	Philippines
437	1977	218	Government of Nigeria	Nigeria
338	1976	216	Government of Nigeria	Nigeria
439	1977	218	Government of Nigeria	Nigeria
440	1977	218	Unknown	
441	1977	218	Impressa Umberto Girola Esrereo	Nigeria
442	1977	218	Belt	Uruguay
443	1977	218	Hongkong & Yaumati Ferry Co. Ltd.	Hong Kong
444	1978	218	Hovermarine Pacific	Japan
445	1978	218	Hongkong & Yaumati Ferry Co. Ltd.	Hong Kong
446	1978	218	Hongkong & Yaumati Ferry Co. Ltd.	Hong Kong
447	1978	218	Hongkong & Yaumati Ferry Co. Ltd.	Hong Kong
448	1979	218	Hongkong & Yaumati Ferry Co. Ltd.	Hong Kong
449	1979	218	Port of Rotterdam	Holland
450	1979	218	Port of Rotterdam	Holland
451	1980	218	Port of Rotterdam	Holland
452	1980	218	Port of Rotterdam	Holland
453	1982	221	Gray Mackenzie	Bahrain
454	1979	218	Maraven	Venezuela
455	1979	218	Maraven	Venezuela
456	1979	218	Maraven	Venezuela
457	1980	218	Hongkong & Yaumati Ferry Co. Ltd.	Hong Kong
458	1980	218	Hongkong & Yaumati Ferry Co. Ltd.	Hong Kong
459	1980	218	Hongkong & Yaumati Ferry Co. Ltd.	Hong Kong
460	1980	218	Jordan Valley Authority	Jordan
461	1980	218	Jordan Valley Authority	Jordan
462	1980	218	Hongkong & Yaumati Ferry Co. Ltd.	Hong Kong
463	1980	218	Hongkong & Yaumati Ferry Co. Ltd.	Hong Kong
464	1980	218	Hongkong & Yaumati Ferry Co. Ltd.	Hong Kong
465	1981	221	City of Tacoma	USA
466	1981	218	Seaspeed Transport Canada	Canada
467	1982	221	City of Tacoma	USA
468	1981	218	Seaspeed Transport Canada	Canada
469	1981	218	Hongkong & Yaumati Ferry Co. Ltd.	Hong Kong
470	1981	218	Hongkong & Yaumati Ferry Co. Ltd.	Hong Kong
471	1981	218	Seaspeed Transport Canada	Canada
472	1981	218	Auto Batam Ferry Service	Singapore
473	1981	218	Hongkong & Yaumati Ferry Co. Ltd.	Hong Kong
474	1981	218	Hongkong & Yaumati Ferry Co. Ltd.	Hong Kong

APPENDIX C: BUILD AND ORIGINAL SALE HISTORY

475	1982	218	Hongkong & Yaumati Ferry Co. Ltd.	Hong Kong
476	1982	218	Hongkong & Yaumati Ferry Co. Ltd.	Hong Kong
477	1982	218	Hongkong & Yaumati Ferry Co. Ltd.	Hong Kong
478	1982	218	Hongkong & Yaumati Ferry Co. Ltd.	Hong Kong
479	1982	218	Hongkong & Yaumati Ferry Co. Ltd.	Hong Kong
480	1982	218	Hongkong & Yaumati Ferry Co. Ltd.	Hong Kong
481	1982	218	Hongkong & Yaumati Ferry Co. Ltd.	Hong Kong
482	1982	218	Hongkong & Yaumati Ferry Co. Ltd.	Hong Kong
483	1982	218	Hongkong & Yaumati Ferry Co. Ltd.	Hong Kong
484	1982	218	Hongkong & Yaumati Ferry Co. Ltd.	Hong Kong
485	1983	218	Britiah Technology Group	UK
486	1983	218	Touristic Enterprises	Kuwait
487	1983	218	Shell Eastern Petroleum	Singapore
488	1983	218	Shell Eastern Petroleum	Singapore
489	1983	218	Shell Eastern Petroleum	Singapore
490	1983	218	Shell Eastern Petroleum	Singapore
491	1983	218	Shell Eastern Petroleum	Singapore
492	1983	218	Touristic Enterprises	Kuwait
493	1983	218	Kedah & Perlis Ferry Services	Malaysia
494	1983	218	Hover Maritime Semandera	Indonesia
495	1984	218	Gozo Channel Express	Malta
496	1984	218	Touristic Enterprises	Kuwait
497	1984	218	Pomas	Malaysia
498	1984	218	Hover Maritime Semandera	Indonesia
499	1984	218	Klassis	Turkey
604		221	Unknown	
605	1985	221	Donau Dampfshiffahrts-Gesellshaft (DDSG)	Austria
606	1986	221	Not Completed	

Other Build - USA:

3001	1974	216	Toryoung - Niagara Falls	USA
3002	1976	216	Hover d'Azur	France

Other Build - HPL (Japan):

203	1979	218	unknown	Japan
204	1979	218	unknown	Japan

Other Build - HM5:

501	1982	527	Sealink Ferries	Hong Kong

HOVERMARINE

502	1983	527	Sealink Ferries	Hong Kong
503	1983	527	Sealink Ferries	Hong Kong
504	1983	527	Sealink Ferries	Hong Kong

Two HM 221 hulls were also built in 1991 in Woolston by Hovermarine International and fitted out . by Textron Marine Systems for the Fire Department of New York

BOOK TWO

Peter White, a field service engineer who spent ten years with Hovermarine, turned out to be a valuable resource for this book, for three reasons. First, readers will come to know his sense of commitment and competence. Second, you will learn the countless number of times he saved and strengthened relationships between the Company and its customers. Third, throughout his employment, he not only kept meticulous diaries; he also saved them. Now, repeated and summarized here, these diaries chronicle in detail some of the most important events of the Hovermarine story—those that took place in the field, around the world.

We found Peter living in semi-retirement in a suburb of San Diego, California, with his Bolivian wife of forty-three years, Wilma. Peter had been thinking of writing his memoirs and we happily offered him this forum.

There were many like Peter White in the Customer Service Department, most of whom Peter knew and worked with, and whose names appear in these pages. These were the men on the front lines, far from the Boardroom....

HOVERMARINE

INTRODUCTION

MY HOVERMARINE ADVENTURE BEGAN ON 9th of August 1976 although the true beginning must be traced back to a friendship that was formed in 1972.

I had been the Engineer/Mate onboard a 100 ton motor yacht based in Antibes, on the French Riviera. When it came time for me to move on from that position my successor was Bill LeMaistre. We stayed in touch during the ensuing years as Bill progressed and finally became the engineering foreman at Hovermarine Transport Ltd. The company was based at Hazel Wharf, Southampton.

I followed my own path through life although Bill and I would meet up whenever I was in town. On one occasion Bill advised me that Hovermarine were looking for a Service Engineer, willing to travel. I applied for the job and was interviewed by John Chapman. We hit it off and I was hired.

My training under the tutelage of Bill Baird was conducted on an HM216 that was being used as a workers' commuter vessel mornings and evenings between the Vosper Thornycroft shipyard in Woolston and Cowes on the Isle of Wight.

HOVERMARINE

CHAPTER ONE

EXPERIENCES

The Philippines, Nigeria, Bolivia, France, Boston, Venezuela, Rotterdam, Tacoma, Singapore, Kuwait, Malaysia, San Francisco

THE PHILIPPINES

With the service engineer's examination under my belt and a newly issued HM2 maintenance license in my pocket, on 27th August, just eighteen days after being hired, I found myself outward bound on a seventeen hour flight to the Philippines.

Little did I know at that time that I was about to spend almost nine out of the next ten years outside of the UK.

I flew from London to Copenhagen, then across Eastern Europe, Russia (passing over Moscow), a refueling stop in Tashkent, where I de-planed just to say I had set foot in Russia, and then on to Calcutta and Bangkok.

On landing in Manila, I reviewed the notes I had taken back in the office in Woolston. I remembered seeing correspondence from Errol McBean and Dave Weston from the Kamalig Inn, in Pasay City. I hailed a passing taxi, and although the driver didn't know the Kamalig Inn, we arrived in Pasay City, and made enquiries and finally arrived. I checked in, showered and prepared for a jet lag induced sleep.

Ten minutes later I was awoken by a knock at the door. It was my new colleagues come to take me to their farewell party which was being held aboard the private yacht owned by the owner of the Bataan-Manila Ferry Services, Gabbi Zosa.

The party was a great success but when I found out that my colleagues were leaving the next day, I was desperate to glean as much information about the operation as possible from them, whereas they were just as desperate to conclude their final business and shopping before their departure. "Don't worry, everything will be all right" was the quote of the day.

The Philippines at that time was under the control of President Marcos, and each night there was a curfew to keep people off of the streets. Anyone caught out after curfew was detained overnight and made to work hard labor the next morning on public service projects. It was not unusual to see street laborers still dressed in their night before party clothes digging trenches or sweeping streets.

The Hovermarine operation was to link Metro Manila, from a berth near the Cultural Center, with the island of Corregidor (Famous American fortress during WWII and now a Pacific War Memorial), and the Bataan Peninsula, at that time a Free Trade Zone.

The company purchased three HM216s to replace a service that had been operated with a Raketa Russian hydrofoil.

Manila to Corregidor was thirty-one miles, and a further nine miles to Bataan. Bataan was at the open end of Manila Bay. The opening of the bay to the South China Sea was thirteen miles across and from that point there was a 2,000 mile reach in a South Westerly direction all the way to Vietnam and Malaysia.

In the design and construction of the Hovermarine craft, aircraft men and ship men had come together to develop a light enough structure to be able to be supported by a cushion of air, whilst being strong enough to withstand the rigors and extremes of operating in an ocean environment. Working at the interface of these two disciplines was to keep me very busy over the next ten years!

The Bataan Manila Ferry Company had scheduled two round trips per day, seven days a week, to Corregidor and Bataan. The third craft was offloaded in Manila on the 30th of November 1976. The craft were named *Sea Express 101*, *102* and *103*.

The *Sea Express* operation started out in a very professional manner. There were six hostesses serving on the craft on shifts, as well as office girls, all of which made going to work more enjoyable for this twenty-six-year-old single male.

Refueling in the beginning was a problem as all the fuel was trucked to the jetty, and then rolled down the ramp in leaky old oil drums, and hand pumped onboard. It was time consuming and a source of fuel contamination.

I spent much of my time, gathering data, writing reports, helping in repairs, and riding around Manila looking for suppliers and suitable shops for skirt repair and replacement skirt segments made with local material.

On the 14th of September we received warnings of the approach of typhoon "Fran." The craft were hastily moved to moorings in the middle of the Pasig River.

After the typhoon passed we decided to take craft 101 across the bay to the shipyard at Bataan for a much needed lift out, maintenance and repairs. As we progressed out towards Corregidor the sea state became increasingly aggressive. One large wave knocked the glass out of the front port passenger loading door, and with free water running up and down the passenger salon, we were able remove the forward stowage locker door and used that to lash across the port door frame and thereby keep much of the seas we were shipping from coming inboard.

As we continued past Corregidor, the forward skirt (the AB Loop) started to tear and flap up onto the deck. The lower segments became detached and streamed aft. As we rounded a headland near to Mariveles the segments were caught in the starboard prop and stalled the engine. The situation was starting to look serious. I apologize now for ignoring protocol, but I took over command at that moment. I re-started the starboard engine and using the engine idle, increased the revs up to 1,200 and slammed the engine into gear.

The segments and cord jamming the prop snapped and we were

able to peel away from the headland just in time. A short while afterwards we were safely alongside at the Bataan Shipyard.

On another occasion whilst crossing the bay the craft hit some debris that broke the forward attachment of the rear air cushion seal, (the "C" loop). We were stranded twenty miles from base. Our valiant Filipino seaman, Ocdol, also the appointed diver, went over the side and we attached some ropes to the loop and hauled it up onto the aft deck. We were amazed that we were able to increase speed to almost normal cruising speed even with a major part of the air cushion system missing.

Time after time incidents like this helped to build confidence, in what was turning out to be a most durable and well-designed vessel.

All too soon my term of contract support came to an end, and on December 28th I was on a plane back to good old UK.

After four months of tropical living I arrived back in Heathrow, with sleet and rain coming down and a National rail strike in progress. Luckily I was able to share a cab back to Southampton.

NIGERIA

After just two weeks in Southampton, on January 12th 1977, I flew out to Nigeria and the start of another adventure.

The first challenging experience with the Nigeria trip was getting the visas from the Nigerian Embassy in London.

The operation with the Federal Ministry of Transport (Inland Waterways Division), was already underway, and I was greeted at the Bristol Hotel in downtown Lagos by Bill Thwaites, Peter Burn, and Dudley Roberts. I was also greeted by another impressive site, as just before my arrival a heavily laden truck had suffered a brake failure on the hill outside of the Bristol Hotel, resulting in the truck plowing into a bus queue at the bottom of the hill and killing several people.

I was about to learn that life here was not quite as precious as in other parts of the world.

On January 14th we all went to the port and assisted in unloading craft HM216-338. After commissioning the craft and helping to set up berthing, workshop space and inventorying the spare parts, some basic training was started.

As a team we bonded pretty well. Bill Thwaites was the rock of the team—solid and dependable.

Robbie liked whiskey, and more than once I watched him getting himself into trouble as he loved to argue with anyone around. On the job he was a completely different person, and I would and did trust my life to him.

During this period Lagos was undergoing a building boom and there was a great demand for cement. Almost every freighter that could float was heading for Nigeria loaded with bags of cement. At any one time there were up to 100 ships laying at anchor outside of the port, waiting for their turn to come in and unload. The unloading was done by hand, with labor gangs carrying the cement, bag by bag, and stacking them on the waiting barges.

Some of the ships anchored outside of the port were attacked by pirates at night, as we heard the reports over the VHF radio. A few of the ships were not all together seaworthy, and seawater got into the cargo holds and turned the cement to concrete. These ships were destined never to leave the West Coast. Some were scuttled and sank at the anchorage.

Lagos city was an incredible collection of eclectic designs and developments. I liked it for the unruly unpredictability and chaos. There were one or two parks of a sort, with giant fruit bats hanging upside down from the trees. Large black and white lizards were common on the street corner garbage tips. It rained at exactly 4:00 p.m. every day with incredible predictability.

The IWD did not seem to be in a hurry to start a passenger service with only one craft, and so we were permitted to run a Sunday service to the resort beaches at Tarqua Bay. The service was so popular, especially with ex-pat families living in Lagos, that the craft was full almost every trip. On some occasions we carried more than a thousand passengers in one day. Of course they all waited for the last scheduled trip to return to Lagos, and so frequently we ended up operating after dark to pick up the stragglers.

On March the 22nd HM218-437 arrived. We soon had the vessel unloaded and continued with training and route proving all around the Lagos area.

One day I was sitting on the dock waiting for the craft to come in, when I noticed that a passenger canoe powered by a large outboard motor had stalled about 400 yards from the shore and was starting to sink. The passengers were getting very distressed. A little way further up the dock was a police launch manned by a constable. I ran to his boat and pointed out the emergency as I started to untie his mooring lines. Looking up I was suddenly faced by the business end of the constable's revolver. A bit more frantic explaining and he caught on to what was happening. I accompanied him as we zipped out to the casualty but before we got there, the HM2 came into view and quickly drew alongside the sinking canoe.

It was a beautiful sight to see the HM2 perform such an effortless rescue and the passengers were easily hauled onboard.

Strangely, neither our success on the Tarqua Bay run, or the timely rescue story ever appeared in the local press.

By April 4th our team was re-enforced by the arrival of Allen Burnett, John Barber and Stan Bullen.

On the 7th of April, Bill Thwaites and I returned to the UK. By this time we had seen eight different corpses floating in the harbor at different times.

I departed from London again for Lagos on June 15th.

By this time the fleet had expanded to three vessels and the team now included Malcolm Beckingham and Ray Norton.

A captain recruited from Florida, Gene Proch, joined us on June 22nd.

New routes were being tried up the Icorudo channel and to Badagari.

It was then decided that a trial service should be tried out in the Eastern River State from Oron to Calabar. This connection could alleviate a traffic congestion that involved a forty-mile trip up to the nearest bridge, by connecting these two towns by a fifteen minute hovercraft trip.

BOLIVIA

The next thing I knew, I was over at the doctors getting all my vaccinations topped up, and then tripping up to London to the Bolivian Embassy! It's funny, I was sure they said *Bavaria*.

November 30th 1977 was the day I flew from London, loaded down with boxes of Hovermarine spare parts, including a full set of Hovercraft skirt segments. The flight was thru Washington D.C., to Panama City Panama, Lima Peru and then on to La Paz.

All baggage had to be claimed in Washington and examined before re-checking on the Panama flight. I struggled up to the inspection desk with my cart piled high. The inspecting officer wanted to know, "What are these?" pointing to the skirt segments. "Rubber skirts," I replied. "Don't try to be funny, Mac," was the response, and so I had to rapidly give a full explanation.

The flight finally arrived at the world's highest International airport, El Alto, near La Paz. As the aircraft doors were opened, I took a gasp of air, and definitely felt a little strange. Could it be the nineteen hours of traveling or the fact that we were now sitting on the Tarmac at the end of a seven mile runway at 13,323 feet above sea level?

In the terminal building and before customs, I met Tony Ossendon, the man instrumental in getting the Hovermarine craft on Lake Titicaca. All the bags and spare parts were whisked through customs as though some pre-agreement had been arranged. As we left the Airport I noticed by the roadside, a giant billboard, with a picture of the HM2 skimming across the lake passing some traditional Inca reed boats.

Within minutes we were on our way across the Altiplano. For some thirty miles we traveled on dirt roads, with scattered adobe and thatched dwellings dotting the countryside, and the snow covered peaks of the Andean range in the background. Arriving at the hovercraft base, a couple of wood framed buildings and a stone walled dock at the water's edge, on the South Eastern corner of Lake Titicaca, this then was Copancara, Bolivia's first International Hoverport.

Hovermarine Titicaca Transport Limited had two craft on site, and they had been in business for more than a year. Getting the craft from the Peruvian Pacific port of Matarani to the Peruvian end of Lake Titicaca had been a tremendous challenge. Even upon arrival at the lake there were further problems involved in launching the craft. The plan was to back the trailers into the lake and simply float the craft off. One trailer became stuck in the mud and is still in the lake to this very day.

One of the major problems with the Bolivian operation was political. Bolivia had had 180 presidents during its first 170 years of existence. Revolution and Coups were a common occurrence and whenever there was a coup the tourists would stop coming.

Once things settled down the tourists would slowly return in small groups, which were insufficient to make operating the hovercraft profitable. With the lowered revenue income, maintenance was allowed to slip, and the craft became unreliable due to neglect. The Bolivian company was unable to make its payments to the European Banks and so I was sent to Bolivia to assist in the overhaul and maintenance on the craft. With improved reliability, it was hoped revenues could be restored to the necessary levels.

Arriving at the lake that day, Tony Ossandon and his leading hand Ricardo Lebon took me on board and started explaining

Photo of the HM2 skimming across Lake Titicaca passing some traditional Inca reed boats

and pointing out all the outstanding faults. My mind started to drift, as the high altitude, and lack of oxygen developed into a pounding in my temples and the beginnings of a terrific headache.

Seeing my distress, Tony suggested that the best cure for altitude sickness was a good night's rest. We were soon back in the car and heading for La Paz.

After a brief visit to the offices of Tony Tours, and with introductions all round, I was taken to the Hotel Gloria. At long last a shower and a clean bed to collapse on! Over the next few days I was able to acclimatize somewhat, first to the altitude, then the change in diet, not to mention that I hardly knew a word of Spanish when I arrived.

I worked on the craft records, trying to get a picture of what had been going on since the Hovermarine team had left. Most days we made the forty-mile trip to the Lake, and we commenced a plan of work based on priorities.

One craft was running and on my fourth day in Bolivia, I joined the craft for the trip to Isla Del Sol, Copacabana, and Puno, Peru. It was beautiful, crossing the lake and I considered myself very privileged to be having this experience. The operation actually gained a mention in the *Guinness Book of World Records*, for the highest operating hovercraft in the world.

My daily routine began around 6:30 am, as I was picked up from the hotel by Ricardo. We would drive up the narrow cobbled streets to the Altiplano where we would stop in La Ciudad del Alto for a breakfast of strong black coffee, with a hunk of bread and Bolivian white cheese. Sometimes we would alternate and stop at a roadside café for api, a grain based hot gruel drink, and pastels, a kind of fried batter covered in sweet syrup and dusted with powdered white sugar. I soon grew very fond of this fare. After breakfast we would pass the police control and toll booth, and drive for the next twenty-five miles on the bumpy dirt road to the lake.

There were quite a few consequences as a result of the high altitude that had to be taken into consideration. Automobiles, (and Hovercraft), were 16% down on power due to the lack of oxygen. The air cushion fans were geared up to run faster, and the passenger configuration was reduced to enable the craft to perform as near to spec as possible.

Once at the Lake work commenced in earnest. We started by removing a failed engine from one craft, and replacing it with a good engine from the other craft. No easy task as we only had a homemade dockside crane with insufficient reach or capacity to lift the engine straight out of the craft. An improvised 'A' frame was constructed to lift the engine onto the aft deck using chain blocks. We then managed to slide the engine ashore along some well-greased planks of wood. As soon as the engine was eased ashore we were able to use the dockside crane to lift it onto an engine cart and remove it to a covered area for strip down.

Another challenge was how to maintain the skirt system. We decided to take the craft to an old dock at the Southern tip of Lake Titicaca called Guaqui. At the dockside I was amazed to see two steam cranes built in the 1920s. They didn't have sufficient capacity to lift the craft, but we figured that we could at least lift one end at a time. The two cranes chugged into position on the dockside and we connected each crane to one of the forward lifting points. I was concerned at this point as to the stresses being set up in the frame of the craft as lifting was supposed to be done vertically using the Hovermarine lifting frame.

The cranes took the strain in tandem, puffed and panted, jerked and shook, and the forward end of the craft came clear of the water. We quickly worked our way into position under the bow, in a small borrowed dinghy, and started changing out the forward skirt segments for those that I had brought from London. Halfway through the operation my heart nearly stopped when the boiler safety valve on one of the cranes suddenly blew off, releasing high pressure steam into the air with a roar. Spurred on to go faster, we quickly finished changing the forward skirt segments, lowered the craft, turned it around and repeated the process for the stern segments.

Some nights I stayed at the lake. We had a good crew, (mostly Aymara Indians) and a cook from Peru. The nights at 12,000 feet above sea level were bitterly cold and the base didn't have much insulation or heating. The dawn was always most welcome.

I was learning Spanish rapidly but with a strange Aymara accent that had my compadres in fits of laughter, and earned me some questioning glances when I spoke Spanish in the city.

December 14th was a very significant day for me. I was to go to the airport with Mario, one of Tony Ossendon's staff, in order to meet Ron Burden, a Hovermarine Accountant, who was flying in from London to re-negotiate the terms of the Bolivian contract.

We arrived at the airport in good time only to find that the flight was delayed. After coffee we were wandering around the arrivals area when Mario was approached by a very attractive young lady, with whom Mario had worked previously. We were introduced, and it turned out that Wilma was a freelance tour guide that had actually brought groups across the lake on the Hovermarine craft. She was waiting for her brother who had been studying in New York and he was on the same flight as Ron Burden. We were soon in deep conversation and I was sad when the delayed flight finally arrived. We exchanged phone numbers, started dating, and were married six months later. We are still married at the time of writing some forty-four years later.

On 18th December it was business as usual at the lake, with a special guest onboard, the British Ambassador to Bolivia.

By the end of January I had developed a relationship with Tony Ossendon; he had set me up with an apartment in the suburb of Sopogachi, given me free use of a Chevy Blazer truck and even offered me a partnership in the business.

It was very difficult to keep the craft running. Spare parts, good facilities and technical support from local sources were in short supply. On one occasion the craft broke down at Puno and could not be repaired there. We proceeded to return to base in Bolivia on one engine, a distance of around ninety miles. We needed some serious engine spares including a crankshaft, in order to get the craft back in service. After phoning various suppliers, and examining options, it was agreed that I should go to the Cummins Factory in Hialeah, Miami. I did so, and arrived back in La Paz on March 7th.

On March 9th I was flying again, this time to Cochabamba, Bolivia, to follow up on a company that was rebuilding a second engine for us. I made a second trip to Cochabamba this time to see our engine run up on a test rig. This turned out to be really exciting as I traveled the 200 miles by the night bus. It took 10 hours on the treacherous roads and I was glad that I couldn't see some of the drop offs as we veered around the hairpin bends, thru clouds of fine dirt and dust.

May 27, 1978 was "D" Day. I passed by Tony Ossendon's office and picked up a telex from Hovermarine asking me to pack up and return to UK as soon as possible. I was a bit pre-occupied that day as I was on my way to the church to get married. After the ceremony and on the way to the reception, I showed my wife our traveling instructions. This was a shock as we had been thinking that we would be in La Paz for at least another year. Fortunately she loved the idea of traveling as much as I did and in the next few days it was a mad panic to get together all the necessary visas and passports that we now required.

On the 3rd of June we set off for New York to visit Aunt and Grandmother, and then on to the UK and the next Hovermarine Adventure.

THE SOUTH OF FRANCE

Nine days in the UK this time, before we were off to the South of France to do some upgrade work on two craft bought by Techniques Avante Garde. The craft were located in San Laurent Du Var on the French Riviera. We arrived on June 20, 1978.

Getting in touch with the TAG representative Guy Bergen proved to be a challenge. We found out that the contract and work had been put on hold whilst all parties concerned did some re-negotiating. We headed back for the UK. I was back in the office in Southampton on August 7th .

BOSTON

The projected operation for the craft was to carry out an experimental hi-speed passenger service, connecting Hingham Shipyard, south east of Boston, with a downtown berth alongside the Boston Aquarium.

The craft lease had been agreed with the Commonwealth of

Massachusetts, and Massachusetts Bay lines were to operate the service for the Commonwealth. The idea was to relieve some of the congestion on the South East Express Way (I-93) and (I-3) and SR-3A, which were all heavily congested, and plagued by large potholes in the winter.

Commuters could drive in from as far away as Cape Cod, and leave their cars for free at the old Hingham Shipyard from where they could take the ferry right into Downtown Boston.

A voyage of ten miles took as little as twenty minutes total by Hovercraft and was an attractive alternative compared with the fifteen-mile road trip, which at peak periods could take up to an hour, plus the hassle of finding somewhere to park once one had arrived in the city.

Mass Bay Lines, under the leadership of Bill Spence and his very able son Jay, had been operating this route with a conventional, displacement catamaran for a number of years.

Having sent reports and faxes from New York, I met up with John Barber again at the Suisse Chalet Motel, in Quincy, MA, which was approximately halfway between Hingham and downtown Boston. It was also conveniently close to the MBTA train, station. We were soon hard at work putting the craft back in order, re-certifying to local US Coast Guard regulations, and repairing some minor stress cracking on the cabin roof.

An interesting point arising out of the Coast Guard inspection was that although our nice compact, self-inflating and covered life rafts were acceptable in Florida, where the waters are warmer, the Massachusetts Coast Guard insisted that we fit square ring life floats with netting in the middle, so that any survivors finding themselves in the frigid waters had to clamber into the netting over the ring and sit in the water until rescued.

For this accommodation, we had to purchase the rafts (four in all, at $430 each), and make substantial modifications to the aft rails, in order to stow the rafts whilst underway.

We had hired some local labor, to assist with these tasks, and performed this work whilst tied alongside Rowes Wharf in Boston. The benefits were that we were able to enjoy a number of different lunch venues, as well as getting to know this beautiful and historic city.

The final inspection and demonstration run for the Captain of the Coast Guard was on November 13th, at which time the craft was signed off as serviceable.

On the 16th of November we ran a demonstration for the Commonwealth of Massachusetts, Department of Public Works. This department was to be in overall control of the craft operations and in the months to come I was to have a lot of interaction with the characters running that office. We would later learn that the Commonwealth of Massachusetts was nearing bankruptcy, and would have to be bailed out by Federal funds in order to keep essential services running.

Amongst the Mass Bay Lines staff we found a diver called Roger Concanon. He was more than willing to help keep the skirt system in tip-top running condition. Roger became our first pilot for training and when he was unfortunate enough to hit a log at speed, thereby damaging the port Impact Blade, a sacrificial piece attached to the leading edge of each hull, we gave him the new nickname of "Chainsaw Concanon."

Right after Thanksgiving, I had to return to UK to have my US visa upgraded. Visas had always been a bit of a grey area on quite a few of my overseas trips, both with Hovermarine and during the years that followed. Anyway, I drove my wife down to New York to hang out with her aunt and family, and I flew from JFK to London on the evening of the 26th of November. I was back in New York by the 29th with my upgraded visa and back on the craft in Boston on the 30th.

During my absence there had been a competition in the local middle schools to come up with a suitable name for the craft. The winning suggestion was *Yankee Skimmer*. There was a naming ceremony and we started to get some press and TV coverage.

By the 11th of December the weather was getting decidedly

colder. There followed a series of trials to monitor the effects of ice buildup on the craft, and the results became the basis of the first HM2 extreme weather operational analysis.

At 28.4 degrees F the waters of Boston Harbor started to produce slush ice floating on the surface. This of course was scooped straight into the engine seawater cooling system and promptly choked the seawater strainers, causing engine overheat. On the vertical sides of the hull the air cushion spray immediately froze, forming an ice sheet that began around mid-ships and grew thicker towards the stern. After one commuter run of twenty minutes, the ice would be as much as eight to ten inches thick. The spray hitting the large life rafts on the aft deck rail formed a lot of heavy ice, which we had to knock off after every trip.

When the snow started falling, it was drawn into the lift fans until a cone of snow and ice was formed, much like a volcano in reverse. Every so often the cone would collapse into the fan with an alarming bang and rattle, but no damage was noted.

A week later the craft was again to show us its adaptability. We had been to a small boatyard (Norwood Marine Inc.), in South Boston, where we could get the craft lifted out to repair the impact blade and replace a damaged rudder. By the time we were due to relaunch, the channel into the yard was completely frozen over. Having broken the ice (which was about six inches thick) near to the dock, we launched the craft and fired up the engines. As we moved forward over the leading edge of the ice, the down pressure of the air cushion displaced the water that was supporting the ice. Great chunks of unsupported ice then broke off under its own weight, thereby opening up the channel. By easing forward over the ice shelf we were able to continue breaking a passage thru the channel one piece at a time. We had soon broken out of the quarter mile channel and were again out in the ice free Boston Bay.

On the 13th of December, the Commonwealth and the DPW (Department of Public Works) had arranged a high profile

The *Yankee Skimmer* in Boston

demonstration of the craft for the benefit of some of the leading members of the Massachusetts Government including State Senator McKinnon.

With everybody expectantly seated onboard, John, following instructions received from Hovermarine Corporation reluctantly had to announce that the trip was canceled, as the deposit for the craft lease had not been received. Amongst embarrassed and red faces from the DPW, the engines were stopped and the keys were removed.

Half an hour later, a messenger arrived direct from the State House and placed a $108,000 check in my hands. The demo was a complete success. The next morning, I was at the Chase Manhattan Bank on Wall Street to deposit the funds into the Hovermarine account.

Meanwhile, the winter drew in and the days got shorter and colder. We continued operating the commuter route up until the end of December. Finally the craft was iced in, and we settled into a routine of keeping vital plumbing from freezing, and running the engines daily to keep the systems operational.

The New Year started at a mild 57 degrees F and raining. We were soon back in business on the Boston Waterfront and on January 2nd 1979 we had Boston's Channel 5 TV onboard. We put the craft through her paces with a run to Hingham, and then some high speed passes for the cameras aboard Mass Bay Lines vessel the *Freedom*. By the 4th of January, temperatures were again back down to 20 degrees F with some substantial icing.

We continued to operate the craft as regularly as the weather permitted. Over the next month we had snow, rain, floods and gales. Every day was different. On one occasion we experienced an ice storm where everything became covered in a cocoon of ice.

We had always been fortunate in meeting nice people wherever we went and Boston was no exception. We were adopted by whole families and never ceased to have an endless round of invitations. One such example was John Schofield, Commercial Attaché at the British Embassy. He invited us to lunch in Boston, and subsequently to visit his home in Sudbury, MA. The Schofields were going on vacation and asked if would stay in their house to dog sit their little terrier "Fiesta." The bonus was that he gave me full use of his Mercedes car complete with the diplomatic license plates.

By this time, Captain John Barber had returned to the UK, and I was left in charge. The Commonwealth of Massachusetts Department of Public Works was becoming unmanageable, and most of our requests for improved dock facilities, spare parts and additional equipment went unheeded. It was then that I came in contact with Martha Reardon from the South Shore Chamber of Commerce. She was a barrel of energy and a great supporter of the commuter craft. She was all for assembling volunteer painters and cleaners to come on board at weekends, which although admirable, made me wonder who was running what.

It was approaching mid-April and it was becoming clear that the DPW was not gearing up for operating the craft through the summer. I had numerous discussions with the Deputy Chief Engineer of the Department of Public Works and Commissioner Terasigni from the Commonwealth Office. They had been stalling on making the lease payments, and had not provided anyone to train to take over from me until April 27th. I was in the middle of a series of messages passing between Hovermarine and the DPW. I made it my priority to clear as many of the outstanding items on the craft and I was asked to assemble and inventory all the spare parts and equipment.

The 25th of May was my last day in Boston, under the current deployment. Next stop: back to LaPaz and the Lake.

BOLIVIA REVISITED

June1st. I visited the offices of Hovermarine Titicaca Transport and traveled out to the lake with Tony Ossendon. Craft 324 had been running most of the year with some success, but craft 311 had been sorely neglected. We fired it up and I took it out for a short test run. I made a lot of recommendations, and wrote up a report, for the benefit of all concerned.

BOSTON REVISITED

July 3rd. Because of the ongoing problems with the Boston operation, I was asked to return to Boston for an update on the current situation there. I was able to talk to Murray Gintis (DPW) on the phone, visit Mass Bay Lines, and discuss the operation and its future, and took lunch with Martha Reardon to judge the operation from the traveling public's point of view.

July 9th. Back in the office in Southampton after an absence of nearly nine months. The following two months were spent preparing for the next overseas adventure, following up on previous operations, assisting with trials, testing, and demonstrating the newest craft.

VENEZUELA

Phew! Hot and sticky was my first impression as my wife and I descended from the inbound New York flight at the Simon Bolivar International airport in Caracas.

In the terminal building we were met by my Hovermarine colleague Pat Nicklen and his wife Marisa, who had just flown in from Brazil. Four hours and a couple of beers later, we were all outward bound again, this time heading for Lake Maracaibo.

Our mission was to provide technical support, training and onsite warranty for the National oil company, Maraven, formerly a Royal Dutch Shell Company. They had just purchased three Hovermarine craft to carry service personnel and equipment out to some of the 500 oil rigs and pumping stations scattered across the surface of Lake Maracaibo.

We landed in the dark, just after a heavy tropical rainstorm. Everything was steaming and sultry as we commissioned two taxis, to haul us and our long stay luggage, the forty miles to Ciudad Ojeda, which was to be our base for the next few months.

Almost two hours later, Pat and Marisa had still not arrived. Finally they turned up, looking both bruised and battered. Apparently their taxi had been involved in an accident.

The next day we were introduced to Pablo Bedini, head of the marine base at Lagunillas, a few miles from the Hotel. Up to this point, Maraven had been operating Old Italian hydrofoils, which were looking severely battered, especially around the stern, as they were used for stern on docking to all the rig installations on the lake.

October 4th. We saw the arrival of our training captain, Ray

Norton, a fellow Brit (More British than most Brits!). We had worked together in Southampton and in Nigeria.

We were taken on a familiarization ride out to the oil rigs on the lake aboard one of the general use launches, of which Maraven seemed to have quite a few. It seems hard to believe now but at this time in 1979, the Venezuelan oil revenue income was estimated at $100,000 per minute.

Just outside of the base at Lagunillas, was the oldest Donkey oil pump in Venezuela. It started pumping out crude oil in 1925 and only stopped working in 1975. How many millions of barrels of crude had been pumped out of this one site could only be guessed at, but one thing for sure was that the surrounding land had sunk as a result of the extraction to such an extent that now the preserved Historic relic was sitting on its own hilltop some 200 feet high.

Out on the lake were many variations in the processes used to extract the crude. Lago Gas 1 was a platform that collected natural gas from the oil deposits below the lake and then compressed the gas to several thousand pounds per square inch, before re-injecting it into the lake bed, in order to force more globules of the heavy crude to the collecting pipes for recovery.

Another drilling barge that we boarded was so intent on keeping to their drilling schedule that a large diesel engine providing hydraulic power to the drill was kept running, even though its cooling water pump had failed. The operator's solution was to play salt water on the external surfaces of the engine from the rigs fire system, and keep the engine running to destruction.

This was the first operation I had been on whereby we were not required to record the amount of fuel we used. In fact, Diesel fuel was cheaper than drinking water.

Within a few days we were set up with students to teach and a classroom to use.

We were welcomed into the administration offices at any

time, for coffee or consultation. The Venezuelans had a love affair with air conditioning as one would step from the 100 degrees F high humidity ambient, into a 65 degrees F chill where all the staff would be wrapped up in jackets and scarves. The coffee was always ready, with a freshly filled thermos flask in every office. The coffee was taken in small plastic cups the size of a whiskey shot, and it was pre-prepared with condensed milk and salt. An acquired taste that I acquired.

Maraven supplied us with a couple of cars and so we had some mobility. My wife and I were off exploring at every opportunity. Some of our favorite trips were to the Guajira markets in Maracaibo, across a spectacular five-mile bridge over the entrance to Lake Maracaibo. At weekends, many of the Maraven people would escape the heat by going up to the resort towns of La Puerta and Merida, between four and seven thousand feet above sea level. Merida had the highest and second longest cable car ride in the world at that time. On one particular weekend we went as far as Cucuta, just over the border into Columbia.

Finally on October 17th, HM218-454 adapted for crew boat work with over the bow loading and unloading, arrived in Maracaibo and was awaiting offloading. The next day, we were onboard assisting the unloading of the craft. This was the first time in my life that I experienced "sunstroke." We had already attached the lifting rig to the craft and I was to stay onboard whilst the craft was hoisted and lowered down to the water, in order to moor the craft alongside and to detach the lifting rig.

The crane took the strain and I was lifted high into the air and out over the ships side. At that point somebody blew a whistle and everything stopped. I was left suspended, not knowing what was going on. The craft was still locked and I did not have the keys. There was absolutely no shelter from the blazing midday sun and I didn't even have any water with me.

Apparently some import documents were not in order and I was left dangling for more than an hour getting hotter and hot-

The Lago Gas 1 platform, Lake Maracaibo, Venezuela

ter before money exchanged hands, and the craft was finally lowered to the water.

Training continued at a good pace for both the mechanics (motoristas) and the Captains. There were some issues with the air conditioning and Pat and I completely re-designed the bow area to make it more rugged for the continual bow on docking.

The craft was ideal for its role. Computer printouts were issued to the craft crew each morning that comprised of a list of oil rigs that had to be visited and in a logical order. Crews were boarded in Lagunillas, with their tools and equipment. The craft would then follow the prescribed route, picking up and dropping off crews at their allocated work stations. Berthing at all the different platforms was made a lot safer with a bow on approach.

Once the craft was in contact with the rig, with the engines slow ahead, the air cushion could be raised or lowered to match the craft height to that of the rig. The work crew could then pass safely over the bow between the conveniently placed hand rails whilst still under the direct observation of the Captain.

I have already mentioned in this narrative as to how visas had always been a problem. Venezuela was no exception. Even the National oil Company couldn't get it right. Every month an agent would come and collect our passports and trip off to one of the many border crossing points to get a fresh entrance stamp valid for a month at a time. Finally, they ran out of border posts, and so one weekend they flew us all out of the country to Aruba and Curacao in the Dutch Antilles, to renew our visas.

Pat was very good to work with on this project and he would often offer to cover any emergencies if we wanted to dash off for a weekend and visit other parts of the country.

In the middle of November we took the night bus from Maracaibo to Caracas. The bus trip itself was an adventure. In the middle of the night near Barquisimeto, everyone on the bus was asleep, even the driver it seemed.

As we came over a rise and started to descend into a valley I could see the floodlights of a new bridge construction up ahead. As we drew closer I could see a large concrete bridge section on a semi-trailer begin to back slowly across our path. The driver failed to re-act as the gap between the bridge section and our line of travel gradually closed.

As we zoomed past, the bridge section hit the bus with a loud metallic tearing sound. The bus driver, now fully awake, screeched to a halt. We all piled out onto the highway to inspect the damage. By a miracle, the concrete section had only hit the last six feet of the bus, but looking at the line of damage it was obvious that if we had impacted even a second or two earlier then there would have been serious injuries to all the passengers on the left side of the bus, which was where I was sitting.

Caracas was beautiful in the city center. We visited the museum of Simon Bolivar, the liberator of many of the South American countries, we watched Sloths slowly and deliberately moving through the trees in the central park (Apparently they normally sleep fifteen to eighteen hours per day), and we ate some great food.

The night bus trip back to Maracaibo was uneventful.

One of the most useful things I was able to achieve whilst working with Maraven was to list their inventory of Hovermarine spare parts and to set up a maximum and minimum stock holding for each part. The materials and purchasing departments would then automatically re-order as stocks were depleted. They continued to purchase parts for at least the next fifteen years.

Interestingly there was an area on the north shore of the lake where we saw a note on the Admiralty Marine Chart that said "Unexplained Phenomena." This intrigued us. For whatever geophysical reason, at this particular location every afternoon there could be seen intense lightning that would persist for an hour or so. There were also still reports of oil workers on the north shores of the Lake being attacked at regular intervals by indigenous Indians armed with bows and poisonous arrows. The tropical forest was very dense in that area.

On the 21st of December we set off on another adventure with Pat's blessing and assurance that he could cover any emergencies. Captain Ray Norton was returning home to the UK and so we dropped him off at Maracaibo Airport before continuing along the coast of the Caribbean Sea to a town called Coro. This area was very desert like, with large expanses of sand dunes. Camels were common around here, and it was very reminiscent of the Middle East.

The next day we traveled along the fabulous Caribbean coastline with its pristine beaches and picture perfect seascapes. Absolutely astounding! We reached Porto Cabello and Valencia, before proceeding to Caracas where we spent the night.

We got an early start the next day, and once again followed the spectacular coastline eastward down past Puerto La Cruz and on to spend the night in the town of Cumana.

Christmas Eve and we were in line very early for the two hour car ferry crossing to La Isla De Margarita. Christmas was fabulous on the Island. There were fiestas, dancing and traditional dress parades everywhere. I remember eating my favorite liver and onions for the main Christmas meal.

All too soon the break was over and we were once again on the ferry. We made it to the city of Barcelona by nightfall, and drove the next day for thirteen hours virtually non-stop to get back to Ciudad Ojeda in time for work on the 28th.

1979 drew to a close in splendid style as we attended a large and festive dance party, with all our new found friends and acquaintances. 1980 continued with more training, keeping the craft operational, and developing a really good reliable service to the oil industry.

When we returned to Southampton, I found that a few things had changed and we were now under the flag of Vosper Hovermarine.

BOSTON AGAIN

By April I was back in Boston, Massachusetts. This time it was to oversee the $100,000 refit of the *Yankee Skimmer* at the giant Bethlehem Steel Shipyard in East Boston.

This was indeed something different, as I had to liaise with a project manager. We held planning and progress meetings in one of the main drafting lofts, surrounded by blue prints of US warships in various stages of design or repair.

As the yard had no experience with Hovercraft or of working in Glass Fiber, I was able to contribute quite a lot towards the overall running of the project.

The summer progressed and we continued to work on the craft which was located on the concrete, on a very drafty corner of the dockyard.

The Massachusetts Bay Lines were running summer bay cruises, and at least twice a day they would pass close to the Hover location and I would hear over the cruise boat's public address system, Norm, Bruce or Jay telling the *Yankee Skimmer* story and introducing me to all the tourists, at which prompting I would take a bow when convenient.

VENEZUELA AGAIN

With the re-fit in Boston almost completed I was asked to return to Venezuela again, and so on August 2nd we were in the air once more, heading for Maracaibo via Newark and Miami. The craft were running reasonably well and by now had logged close to 500 power hours each.

We stayed until August 12th, analyzing craft performance, spares consumption and service histories, as well as carrying out some refresher training.

BOSTON AGAIN

By late afternoon on the 12th we were back in Boston, and the next morning I zoomed back to Bethlehem Steel, half expecting to see the craft in service. There had been some issues regarding the engine performance as the company re-building the motors would not accept liability for returning the fuel pressures back to their pre-strip down settings without the owner's permission. As the craft was on charter, this decision had to be referred back to Hovermarine.

The following day, I checked out of our hotel and took our luggage with me to Bethlehem Steel. Spent all day onboard and in discussions with the DPW and conducting sea trials, and finishing off odd outstanding jobs. Leaving the craft late, I arrived just in time at Logan Airport to meet my wife and to catch our night flight back to London.

ROTTERDAM

Between September 1st of 1980 and the end of the year I made three trips to give technical assistance to our support team in Rotterdam on the Havendienst Port Patrol Boats. The work was hard at times, and the east wind was bitterly cold as we worked some skirt and hull repairs at night.

These craft were on service on average fifteen hours per day, often at low speeds which caused extra wear and tear on the skirt systems. Debris in the water counted for the rest of the damage that was caused to the hull, skirts and propellers.

Rotterdam was a fascinating place to work. With over 300 ship movements per day there was always something interesting going on. I have never met a Dutchman that I didn't like and in addition to that they made great coffee that was available at any time.

One of my official side trips from Rotterdam was to visit an early Hovermarine craft (315) called *Kallo* down in Antwerp, Belgium, that had been built as a harbor maintenance craft.

Wheelhouse of *Havendienst 9* during trials. *L to R*: Derek Stevens, Trials Manager; Dave Weston, Captain; Stan Bullen, Operations Engineer

BOLIVIA

1981 started off with a continuation of our world travels. By January 3rd we were off back to Bolivia, where once again I became involved with the Hovermarine craft on Lake Titicaca. The interest this time was that there were some potential buyers that may have been interested in taking over the operation. I assisted with reviewing the major problems on the craft and then flew over to Lima Peru to pay a courtesy visit, but in the end nothing developed.

VENEZUELA

The 8th of March we were back in Maracaibo to visit the Maraven operation. I was able to help out on a number of craft problems, including changing a rear skirt loop one night. We reviewed all the craft running records and made recommendations. I was also asked to compile some potential sales propaganda material to aid future Hovermarine sales. By the 21st of March, I was back at Hovermarine in Southampton ready to start on the next project.

TACOMA FIREBOAT PROJECT: APRIL 1ST 1981 – APRIL 21ST 1983

What a privilege it was to be involved in what were and remain most undoubtedly the world's most sophisticated fire boats. These vessels had everything a firefighter could desire, from a waterborne point of view. High speed (31 knots), high pumping capacity (7500 gpm with all three pumps running), six monitors that could deliver water to a fire up to 400 feet away, a medical bay, high access ladder, AFFF foam capability, highly maneuverable stable work platform, and all capable of being operated by a crew of two.

Our potential for future sales in the US market were very good as at this time there were only thirty-nine dedicated fireboats in operation in the whole country, and most of these were based on slow tugboats, with limited firefighting capability.

My roles were multiple, from liaising between design and build, assisting writing service manuals and training programs, and once the craft was launched, being fully involved in hundreds of hours of continuous pumping trials. I somehow became king of the fire officer's panel, and as it worked out Derek Stevens and I were the only ones in the company that became fully conversant with all aspects of the fire system controls.

The craft had three large intakes for the fire pumps located on the flat underside of the hull between the sidewalls. The intakes were isolated by hydraulically operated butterfly valves which were in turn electrically controlled from the fire officer's panel. A vacuum was created in the fire main using a Bendix vacuum pump from an aircraft braking system. When sufficient vacuum was created the sea valves could be opened and the water would then flood in to prime the fire pumps. The outflow from the pumps could then be directed to any or all of the monitors via electro hydraulically operated valves controlled from the fire officer's panel. The monitors could be swiveled 270 degrees left and right, and 270 degrees up and down, and the nozzles could go from a straight jet to a ninety-degree spray. Even now I can feel my enthusiasm for the craft being regenerated.

We had some more practical demonstrations of the craft's capability during this period. One of these was to play our high access ladder and monitor against the side of a VLCC that was moored alongside the local refinery at Fawley. In the photo on the next page, that's me operating the boom!

Another demo and photo opportunity was when we wanted to set fire to an old barge loaded with bails of kerosene soaked straw. The Port of Southampton was not too keen on having a blazing barge drifting around in their jurisdiction and so we were obliged to have the barge towed to outside of the port limits. At the appointed time the blaze was set, the fire boat came zooming into site and pumping commenced. I used one of the deck monitors to do most of the work and we soon had the situation under con-

Tactical demonstration of a Tacoma fireboat

trol, but as it turned out bails of straw are very hard to extinguish remotely as the inner core of the bails keep smoldering long after the flames are extinguished. We continued to pump water until all were satisfied that a re-ignition was not going to occur.

Now came the difficult part. We were supposed to take the barge in tow and haul it back to the Itchen, but now the barge was so heavy with so much water inboard that we could not make any headway against the freshening afternoon breeze. In addition we could not pump the barge out as the shredded and burnt straw embers kept blocking our pumps. After our second tow line broke, we were obliged to call in a local tow company who came and saved the day.

Although I was officially assigned to the Tacoma project, there were plenty of small diversions with delivery runs from

Southampton to the English East Coast Ports and to mainland Europe, as well as several more support missions to our team in Rotterdam.

In Mid-April I was involved in delivering craft 465, named *Defiance*, from Southampton to the port of Flushing in Holland where the craft was loaded on a ship bound for Vancouver, Canada.

The whole of the month of May was spent on trials and testing of craft 452 for the Port of Rotterdam, culminating in an extended delivery run from Southampton to Rotterdam with stop-overs in Brighton and Dover, arriving in Rotterdam on the 29th of May.

At the end of June I was once again back in Rotterdam to assist the team and to carry out some warranty repairs.

The remainder of 1981 was a mélange of Tacoma testing, sea trials on new builds, and continuing with the Tacoma Manuals. We all worked right through the Christmas holidays, apart from the 25th.

1982

January 13th saw me on yet another delivery run on craft 474, a standard HM218 passenger craft bound for HYF in Hong Kong. This time the port of embarkation was Le Havre in France.

By April all the trials and testing were complete and the Tacoma Fire Boat *Commencement* (467) was prepared for the sea journey from Southampton to Rotterdam via Vlissingen and the Dutch canals. This was the first time out in the open sea and we were pleased that the craft maintained all the good sea keeping characteristics of a standard HM2.

We picked up a heavy swell coming in from the Atlantic, after a recent storm and between Beachy Head and the White Cliffs of Dover; we were surfing down the face of the waves, steering like mad to keep on course before whooshing into the trough of each wave and applying power to climb out and over the next wave. Once we had rounded Dover we were again in the lee of the land.

We crossed the English Channel at a shallow angle and arrived in Vlissingen after a seven-and-a-half-hour crossing. The next morning we proceeded at a more leisurely pace, through the canals to the Port of Rotterdam. Our only concern on this leg of the journey was of being crushed between some of the enormous barges that crammed into the locks with us, every time there was a water level change.

By April 27th *Commencement* was safely loaded in the hold of a freighter, and was off on its extensive journey, through Panama and up the US west coast to Tacoma.

It was time for a little vacation for my wife and I. We flew to Boston to visit friends, drove to New York to visit family, flew to San Francisco, bought an old Ford Pinto, and then drove the 855 miles all the way up the coast to Tacoma.

This may be a good place to acknowledge the extraordinary skills, innovativeness and dedication of some of my fellow workers at Woolston. Whilst fully acknowledging the amazing contributions made by all, I would like to devote a few lines to those who built the craft and those that brought the craft to the customer.

The operations department, initially run by John Chapman, and then by Peter Hill and Vaughan Turland was all dependent on the operations team to get the job done.

Bill Thwaites, Senior Captain, was a leader of men. He was solid and unshakeable in his resolve. I first met Bill in Nigeria and then worked for three months with him in Saudi Arabia. Bill had been a ship's captain in the Merchant Navy, and he made regular runs from the UK to South America on the Royal Mail Lines ships, hauling cargo as varied as hardwood lumber from the Amazon, to rail road tracks and locomotives from the industrial heart of Britain. He had no sense of smell, which made life particularly dangerous when entering confined spaces on-

L to R: Eaon Furnell, two visiting Tacoma City Councilmen, Ron Lewis (Shipwrights foreman), Colin Atkinson (engineer foreman), and Chief Mitchell

board ship. He was fondly known by the team as "Father." After the Hovermarine days he went on to become a High Speed ferry operative on the Southampton to Isle of Wight route.

Dudley Roberts (Robbie), was the Senior Service Engineer. Robbie was of Anglo-Indian origins and he would often enthrall us with stories of his early life running a steam engine power plant on a tea plantation in Nepal. When he married Marge, he was driving large copper ore carrying trucks from the mine to the railhead. They would travel together and he would tell the story of sleeping in a tent beneath the truck, only to be awoken by a large tiger prowling around their campsite. We went on to have quite a few adventures with Robbie, in Nigeria, Malaysia, Holland, and many other locations where our paths crossed, if only for a short while. He had a great smile and a gentlemanly attitude towards everyone.

From the manufacturing plant a couple of people stand out for exceptional skill and devoted loyalty to the company.

One such person was Ray Sturgis. He hand-painted every single craft that was built with such skill that you would swear that it had been sprayed. Customer designs and logos never fazed him, and the finished job was spot on and very long lasting.

Another such person was Tony Jackson. He had a great skill with neoprene and a sewing machine, and he continued producing skirts, segments, and loops for the craft long after the official Hovermarine banner was taken down. In all my assignments I never found a manufacturer that could produce a similar product anywhere near the quality of those made by Tony Jackson.

To pay tribute to all my past colleagues will not be possible in these pages, but I acknowledge the honor it has been to serve with such a valiant team.

TACOMA

Memorial Day, 31st May 1982. There may have been as many as fifty firetrucks—ladder companies with ladders fully extended and flying giant Stars and Stripes, paramedic vans, and police cars, all with their flashing lights and sirens blasting away. There were popcorn and hotdog sellers, and helium filled balloons escaping the hands of small children. The sun was shining and Commencement Bay was calm. The focus of all this activity was centered around the Ruston Way pier and fireboat station on the south shore.

Just after noon appeared a new vision to the fire fighting world as the world's first Hovercraft fireboat roared into site at a startling 31 knots.

After a large arc across the bay, Captain John Barber, skillfully brought the craft to a dead stop, 200 yards off of the fireboat station.

I was sitting at the fire officer's control panel, and for a full ten seconds my mind went blank as to what had to be done next. "Don't Panic!"

Recovering rapidly, and having already vacuumed down the fire main, I had water at the monitors in under a minute, we continued to give a full demonstration of the crafts capabilities, from the under dock monitors, full jet and full spray from the Stang deck monitors, and then the most impressive full flow of all three pumps, thru the main monitor, throwing 7,500 gpm over 450 feet in a powerful arc thru the sky that could easily sink any small craft fool enough to pass under the deluge.

Finally, after about a five minute pumping display, I had to bring the show to a close, due to an overheating pump clutch bearing. As we came once again back onto hover, and started to drain out the fire main, we received a radio call asking for more pumping which we reluctantly had to decline. We took off across the bay, and did one large arc before returning to alongside at the Ruston Way fire station.

Once alongside, it was smiles and congratulations all around. My wife had been with the local VIPs and fire officers on a nearby hillside, and she said it was the proudest day of her life.

Following the reception of the craft, we were all invited to the house of Owen Douglas. Owen was a consultant to the Tacoma Fire Department, and he virtually built the spec for the fire boat around the HM221 platform. He was also working on a prototype air bed for the treatment of severe burns victims.

The craft had only arrived in Tacoma six days earlier and in addition to John Barber coming over to work his magic, Hovermarine had also sent a young fitter from the engineering department called Keith Rood. He was to prove invaluable over the next few weeks.

We soon settled down to a training regime as well as keeping on top of all the requirements of this fairly sophisticated craft. There were a lot of US certification and performance checks to go thru which kept us on our toes. Fuel consumption trials, exhaust emission trials, noise level trials, the list was endless.

The world's first hovercraft fireboat, *Defiance*, on Commencement Bay en route to an inauguration ceremony for the City of Tacoma

We based ourselves at the fire boat station under the 11th Street Bridge in downtown Tacoma.

The crews we worked with were some of the best guys you could ever hope to meet. Three of the men had been on introduction trips to Southampton and already had a good base knowledge of the craft. Monte Harrison, Jim Nelson, Ron Shouse, Harold Strong, and Garry Tennison were amongst the principal operatives at the beginning, whereas Garry Yotter and his right-hand man, John Rawlins, were in charge of maintenance for the new craft as well as much of the remaining fire department equipment.

We became good friends with all the crews, and would socialize after work and at weekends and our wives were always off on trips together whenever possible.

Garry Tennison taught us scuba diving and this was a sport that kept my attention for the next thirty years, as well as providing another asset for Hovermarine. Our friendship continues to this day.

To give an example of the generosity of these great Northwesterners I must recount the following. My wife and I had tired of hotel life and so we took on a lease on an unfurnished apartment just across the carpark from the Tacoma Mall. Somehow word got out that we needed furniture and soon the firetruck radios were humming all over Tacoma. Within one day we had the entire place furnished and a spare room stacked with stuff that we could not use.

As we continued with the craft acceptance trials, the program was interspersed with numerous demos for parties as diversified as the National Union of Fire Fighters, Seattle City Council, and Port Officials from Honolulu and Catalina. Sometimes we would do as many as four demos in a day. There was a series of filming runs, and on one occasion we actually pumped some water on a smoldering barbeque that had not been properly extinguished.

All too soon we were flying out of SEATAC, back to London. Within a few days we were fully involved in the trials and testing of the second Tacoma fireboat in Southampton, an activity that kept us busy up to the end of the year 1982.

1983

January, mid-winter, and we were anxiously looking for a weather window to get the second Tacoma fireboat across the channel and up to Rotterdam to catch the west-bound freighter.

By January 11th we were ready for the dash to Holland to meet the shipping date, but at the first attempt we were turned back by bad weather. On the 13th we tried again and this time we managed to get as far as Dover before the weather again made us dive for cover.

We finally made it to Vlissingen on the 16th and had the craft stowed onboard by the 18th.

The second fire boat arrived safely on February 24th and another round of acceptance and performance trials was commenced.

Some of the trials were conducted on behalf of MARAD (United States Maritime Administration). Craft 467 was recorded at 31 knots at a fuel consumption of 61 USG/Hr.

I've mentioned how generous the Tacoma folks were to my wife and me. When we arrived back in Tacoma for our second tour of duty, our dear friend Garry Tennison took control and invited us to stay at his house out at Gig Harbor. He and his wife Penny treated us like royalty, loaned us his new car, took me diving on numerous occasions, and taught us a lot about life outside of the city.

On March 24th both craft went on a joint operation to aid a Korean ship that was flooding and in danger of capsizing in the City Waterway. The fireboats used the craft eductors, and continued pumping all night until the flood levels were reduced to a safe level.

On the 24th of April we flew back to London.

Once back at Hazel Wharf I quickly became involved with assisting with some of the trials on the largest Hovermarine craft to date, the HM527, craft number 503. I also assisted on trials and testing of some standard HM218 craft (craft number 468 in particular which was being shipped to Canada).

It was funny at times, when people back at the office would ask if I had just joined the company, as we had never met before.

SINGAPORE

There was trouble in paradise. Our clients at Shell Singapore had an ongoing technical problem that they could not solve and our man on the ground, Trevor Lewis, was threatening to quit.

By 11th of June I was on my way east, via Muscat and Kuala

Lumpur to Singapore. I checked into the Cockpit Hotel and set off the next day to tackle the problems at Palau Bukom.

There were plenty of craft problems caused by the high ambient temperature and the high utilization of the craft but this was aggravated by personal conflicts between the SEPL Marine Manager, Colin Stewart, and our man Trevor Lewis. Within two days Trevor had quit and I started to build bridges.

I worked very hard over the next few weeks, especially on one craft that had an intermittent problem on the cooling system that was finally traced back to an original build error.

25th of June. The Bukom Island refinery was inaugurating its brand new Hydro-Cracker. All the top managers and VIPs from Shell were coming, and we had all three Hovermarine running beautifully, with their Air con systems running at maximum. Colin was in his element as he took up position in the wheelhouse of the lead craft winging over to Bukom; he had the other pilots fly their craft in close formation.

At the end of June, Colin Stewart's tour of duty came to an end and his replacement was Mike Whichellow, who was also a former sea captain. Mike and I shared an interest in diving and we went on several dives in the balmy waters around Singapore over the next few months. We stayed friends with Mike and Mary and even visited them at their home near Plymouth in the UK.

By the 28th of July, John Barber was off back to the UK, and we speculated where we would meet up next as I accompanied him to the airport.

BACK TO ENGLAND

August 17th. My wife and I returned to the UK with a thousand stories and a good suntan. We were very popular at parties.

At the time, craft number 485 (a standard HM218 passenger craft) was being chartered to a company called Wightlink. They were operating a passenger service out of Portsmouth to Ryde on the Isle of Wight, a very popular route, especially through the summer. I provided technical support from Hovermarine and kept on top of the maintenance. All was going well until one windy afternoon the captain of a Navy Minesweeper HMS *Kellington* misjudged his turn within the harbor and his ship crushed the HM2 against the dock.

KUWAIT

Running parallel to this job was the completion and delivery of Craft 492, the second of three craft bound for Touristic Enterprises in Kuwait. Once the trials and testing were completed, we made the delivery run from Southampton to Rotterdam a process I was becoming very familiar with.

I flew out to Kuwait on 12th November and met another one of the larger-than-life characters, our agent Ron Hughes. He invited me to stay in his apartment along with his giant Irish wolfhound. Apart from the fact that one could hardly get into the bathroom because of all of his home brew kits bubbling away, everything else was just fine. The service ran well until 1990, when Iraq invaded.

Craft 492, the second of three craft bound for Touristic Enterprises in Kuwait

I was back in London by November 28th, and returned to general duties at Hovermarine until the end of the year.

1984

We were still busy at the Hovermarine Plant, and I was involved with many different projects at the same time.

On the 7th of April, SEP Singapore were in trouble again. A craft had suffered a serious accident, and a lot of bow damage was reported. I flew out this time with Tony Squibb, one of Hovermarine's leading Glass Fiber technicians. We went straight to work upon arrival. We had to remove the forward skirt system from an undamaged craft in order to make a mold for the repair.

I carried on stripping out all the lift machinery, steering, fan drives, lift engine, in fact everything that was in the forward engine bay. I worked with Tony cutting out all the damaged area, it was murder as the tiny glass fibers found their way into our open pores, even showering brought very little relief and the initial laying down to sleep was like being on a Fakir's bed of nails.

We worked like Trojans and had the repair all boxed up in record time by 10th of May. Tony returned to London on the 11th whilst Hovermarine had other plans for me.

PALAU PELANGI (MALAYSIA)

I met with Graham Gifford for dinner in the Hyatt Hotel in Singapore and he was able to brief me a little as to what was going on.

The next day I flew to Penang and then transferred to a twin-engine island hopper that took me out to Palau Langkawi (Rainbow Island), right on the Thai-Malay Border.

Robbie had set up the single craft operation for Kedah & Perlis Ferry Services, and all was going well, with good passenger numbers, the craft being full almost every trip.

Palau Langkawi was indeed a paradise island. It had jungle, rubber tree plantations, terraced rice paddies and beautiful sandy beaches. I was loaned a small Honda 50cc motorcycle that enabled me to tour around a little, and I had adventures with a very large, horned water buffalo, very reminiscent to that famous finger waggling scene from the movie *Crocodile Dundee*. Another time I returned from a challenging afternoon spent on the beach, trying to avoid a troupe of wild monkeys only to find that I had inadvertently brought an unfriendly snake back to my room in my rucksack.

18th of June. The craft impacted with some debris and came limping home with some serious propeller vibration. We hastily loaded spare parts and equipment and made plans to go to the nearest slipping facility, which was over the border into Thailand near a town called Satun.

It turned out that there were some restrictions about Europeans entering Thailand by sea, and so as the craft set out for Satun I went north to the Thai border, where I had to walk a half mile or so across no-mans-land before being able to present my passport at the Thai border. From the border I rode a local tuk-tuk to the southern Thai city of Hat Yai.

The next day was another surprise, as I observed the early morning, orderly file of saffron robed, Buddhist monks, from the oldest to tiny little three- and four-year-old boys, all carrying brown clay pots. As they passed thru the market all the traders were passing out samples of their produce until the monks' pots were full.

The journey out to Satun was a long ride in another tuk-tuk about twenty-five miles. I enjoyed very much intermingling with the local population, and observing as the driver swerved to miss various snakes that crossed our route.

The "shipyard" was something else. It had come into existence at least a couple of hundred years ago, and it had been used almost exclusively for the building and repair of traditional wooden fishing boats.

We set to work modifying the slipping trolley and finally had it all blocked out ready for the HM2. As we hauled the craft up the slope it rained, and rained in such a deluge, that we were standing in ten inches of water on the surface of the seven degree incline, with all kinds of jungle debris, dead animals and insects sluicing past.

We replaced the damaged propeller but also noticed severe damage to the rear skirt system. We replaced the complete assembly. The craft was re-launched. We found that we could pay a fee that enabled me to leave Thailand by sea, thus avoiding the long land trip back to Langkawi.

The craft was quickly cleaned up and put back into service. The ridership was undaunted, and over 2,500 passengers were carried over the next three days.

It was time to go home. Back in England things were still moving right along. It turned out that the company had won a contract to supply a charter vessel to Harbor Bay, a business park development located on Bay Farm Island, just to the north of Oakland Airport in California.

Craft 485 had already been re-painted in the Harbor Bay livery.

My old friend John Barber was to be the charter captain, but there was a problem. Late in 1983 John had undergone open heart

HM2 485, in its new livery, being launched at the Woolston Works: destination San Francisco

surgery. The CAA (Civil Aviation Authority) were willing to re-instate John's operational license, provided that he was accompanied by a certified co-pilot, a rank that had never existed before.

I soon took and passed the Hovermarine Captain's License, the CAA Private Pilot's Medical, the Department of Trade Navigation Certificates, UK Radio-Telephony License, plus Hovermarine's type rating on the HM216 and the HM218.

1985: SAN FRANCISCO

We arrived in San Francisco to a very warm welcome and we moved into the Coral Reef motel in Alameda.

Ron Cowan, the developer of Harbor Bay, was a dynamic entrepreneur with varied interests, including a radio station, the business park development and a video conferencing center. He also flew his own helicopter, until an ill-advised crash one foggy morning.

Ron's son, Scott Cowan, also worked for the organization and amongst other things operated a small (six seat) amphibious hovercraft. Ron had also hired a marine transportation consultant—ex-Golden Gate Ferries manager Stan Kowleski.

It turned out that the reason that the Hovermarine craft was well suited to Ron Cowan's plans was all because of the migratory route of the sturgeon fish. Apparently all the sturgeon would annually migrate along the north shore of San Francisco Bay, either on their way to or coming from the breeding grounds up the Sacramento River. Because of this, the environmentalists would only allow Ron to put in a few pilings to secure a floating pontoon dock, connected to the beach by a long gangway, on a temporary basis. There was to be no dredged channel permitted, which ruled out almost any other type of vessel, especially as the bay around the business park was quite shallow.

The craft was an immediate success. The Harbor Bay team would arrange for half day tours for interested business groups, city councils, chambers of commerce, investors, bankers—in fact, anyone that wanted to come and see the business park, or

On the pier in San Francisco with the scheduling and hospitality crew. Captain John Barber is in the foreground, left. Peter White is on the far right. Third from right is Scott Cowen

just ride on the hovercraft. An appointment would be made, and we would hover over and pick up the respective group and take them to the Harbor Bay dock.

The craft was fitted with a TV monitor that displayed a promotional video for every group as they came onboard. After a while we got to know the video word perfect, especially some of the more colorful phrases such as, "Hovermarine, located in the Silicon Valley of hovercraft technology."

There were always two of the Harbor Bay girls on every trip, and we all became firm friends. The girls would accompany the tour around the business park whilst John and I would sit at the dock awaiting the party to return.

In the early days we did a lot of promotional trips for video opportunities—under the Golden Gate, looping around Alcatraz, and up and down the San Francisco waterfront. At weekends and on Public Holidays we were asked to give free rides out of Pier 1 on the Embarcadero. We met an amazing assortment of people, from a couple that wanted the captain to marry them, to one gentleman who was ninety-six years old, possibly the oldest passenger ever to ride on a Hovermarine craft.

We had based the craft at Ballena Bay Marina, right next to Alameda. It was very convenient especially after a few weeks on site, when Wilma, Elaine, and I took a month-by-month rental on an apartment just around the corner. We had everything we needed in Ballena Bay, from fuel to toilet pump outs, a deli, and the Whales Tail bar and restaurant with its magnificent views across the San Francisco Bay.

By November, we went into a month of thick fog. Harbor Bay was offering sightseeing tours of the San Francisco waterfront, starting from the Harbor Bay Dock. On occasion we would load the craft, zoom off into the fog, and do a huge loop in the middle of the bay and return to Harbor Bay. Occasionally someone would ask why we hadn't gone to San Francisco and we would reply that if we had, "You just wouldn't see it.

Sometimes we would get a shock in the fog when a large target would suddenly appear on the radar shooting across our course which would turn out to be aircraft taking off from nearby Oakland Airport.

Along with the promotion, we ran some more serious trials for MARAD, the U.S. Coastguard and Navy. We even did a military evaluation for three months during which we had to carry an Army rifle in the wheelhouse. We picked up groups from all over the Bay Area, bound for Harbor Bay. From Vallejo and Richmond in the north; San Rafael, Tiburon, and Sausalito in the Central Bay area; and then from down south, we went all the way to Redwood City and San Mateo.

As 1985 was running out we realized that much as we liked this location, it was not going to last forever. On January 15th, 1986 the Harbor Bay Charter came to an end.

1986

We loaded our most reliable Craft 485 on the 20th of March, and with heavy hearts we left the Bay Area.

Back in Southampton, all was not well. The company had shrunk dramatically.

We trickled along, assisting with ongoing concerns from previous customers. On the 18th of April we drove up the English east coast to the port of Felixstowe, and John and I made one last six-hour trip together in Harbor Bay Craft 485 around the coast back to Southampton.

I was laid off from Hovermarine on May 23rd. Was that the end of my Hovermarine story?

No way! Within one week I was back in Singapore on another repair job for SEPL. I formed my own company, Hawthorne Marine Services, and continued to be involved on and off with Hovermarine craft over the next twenty years.

After the dust had settled at Woolston, Peter Hill, Allen Burnett, and Graham Banks picked up the pieces.

CHAPTER TWO

MAJOR TRIPS

*Nigeria: Lagos to Calabar. USA: Cape Canaveral to Boston.
Europe: Southampton (UK) to Oslo (Norway)*

WEST AFRICAN HOVERCRAFT MARATHON LAGOS – CALABAR, JULY 24 – JULY 29 1977

Craft: Hovermarine HM2 439
Crew:

E. Proch	Capt.
Mr. Akiou	Capt. Pilot
Mr. A.O. Subou	Qtr. Master
P. White	Engineer
M. Sampou	Engineer
Alhagi Musa	Seaman
Agoona Nama	Seaman

HM2 439 known as Hovercraft *Innovator III* was withdrawn from normal passenger service in Lagos on Sunday 17th July, in order to make necessary preparations for the trip to Calabar.

Ten, forty-five-gallon oil drums were stowed inside, after removing the forward seats port and starboard, and four seats each side amidships. This gave us a total capacity of 650 gallon of fuel, for which, later we were to be very grateful.

Of course in keeping with all great expeditions, finance was a setback, and it wasn't until Thursdaythe 21st (initially our departure date) that we received N 1000 (*Naira*) with which to purchase such necessary items as cooking stoves, food, beds, mosquito nets etc.

We left the choice of crew to our pilot, Capt. Akiou, and initially we were alarmed to hear that he required three additional men. However time was to show that experience counts.

Long before dawn on Sunday 24th July I crawled from my bed, gathered my bags and prepared to leave. At Ijora all was ready by 06:00 except for the arrival of our Pilot Capt. Akiou.

At 08:00 ropes were slipped, skirts were blown and we eagerly surged over hump* into the unknown. Under the Eko and Carter bridges, up the Icorodu channel and out across Lagos Lagoon where an early morning mist obscured all sight of land. We soon found Balava Island using radar, and once past, the way was clear to Epe and Leke.

Once past Epe we were in new territories, but Capt. Akiou bounded along with confidence. The way was fairly wide most of the time; 150 ft with river grass each side giving an impression of wide water meadows which gave away to more dense vegetation on the true river banks.

Around 11:00 we stopped at a rickety wooden jetty in a small village for the crew to purchase food whilst Sampou and I took time out to clean raw water filters. I was surprised as time passed at how proficient Mr. Sampou became at cleaning filters. As soon as the engine stopped we would race each other for the engine room. The whole process took less than two-and-a-half minutes from engine stop to engine start.

By 11:30 we were off again, zooming along quite wide waterways at full speed and then suddenly shooting off at right angles down some obscure, narrow twisting creek, and each mile looking like the last—jungle and river grass lining the banks, with creeks

---

*Over hump: When a hovercraft's speed exceeds the rate at which the air cushion displaces the water beneath the air cushion and the craft rises up to ride on the surface of the water with minimal displacement.

and rivers joining and leaving at all angles. Occasionally we passed villages where local natives would rush from their houses, mouths open in amazement. An expression that changed to joy as we exchanged waves and then horror as our wake smashed up their flimsy moorings and canoes and tore beneath their stilted houses.

At 13:00 we tied up at a slightly larger than small village to prepare some lunch, at the same time Sampou and I transferred 514 liters of fuel into the tanks and generally checked around the machinery.

Lunch over, we were off again, twisting and turning, going in no particular direction at all. At one point we hove too and closed in on a passenger boat that looked like a wooden hull with several garden sheds precariously mounted on the gunnels.

There was much horn blowing and waving as it turned out that Captain Akiou's daughter was aboard, on her way to Lagos for the vacations. As the boat drew alongside we could see up to 100 people crammed onboard. A bemused little girl was pushed forward and Akiou handed her some money.

With a twinkle of a tear in his eye he proudly told us that he had not seen this daughter for two years as she has been living with relatives. We were all suitably impressed as he told us of his other twenty-one children and it was hard to keep his attention on the river as he frequently turned around and used both hands to illustrate this or that point.

By 15:00 the river had narrowed down considerably, at times less than two boat widths. The jungle was more dense and ominous with the tall trees blocking out most of the light. The water was black and brackish resenting the intrusion of our bow wave. Our horn tone echoed eerily about us as we negotiated tighter and tighter bends, seeming to completely double back on many occasions.

At one such corner, for corner it certainly was, we simply ran out of river and had to go frantically astern to avoid hitting the opposite bank. It was just past this point that we passed over a small floating island of weeds, unable to avoid it in the narrow passage.

Suddenly all port side intakes indicated blockage and the port engine tacho gave a sickening plunge to zero. Our little island had decided to come along for the ride.

Gene took the controls and tried to maneuver so that the AB could get a line on a tree, but to our surprise we discovered that the apparently stagnant water was running a five knot current. With only one engine and no lift we were helpless and so an anchor was hastily prepared.

With one anchor and all the chain gone we were still proceeding stern first unimpeded. The second anchor was dropped and within another 200 yards the craft came to a halt.

The seamen were first in the river with knife and hacksaw whilst I used the boathook to force some of the island out of the "D" loop. The boys were having a hard time and when Alhagi surfaced downstream and had to swim for his life to get back, we streamed a line well astern for them to grab.

Subou and Akiou then entered the water and all took turns diving and cutting at the enmeshed vegetation.

It is strange how in a dense forest, voices keep echoing from the trees, for this was the only sound to be heard. The forest seemed as dead as my engines at this moment.

The little island was so fond of hovercraft it just would not let us go. Finally Alhagi stood on the half submerged mass and using the boathook as a punt pole against the transom, managed to get us free.

These men were all experienced river hands and they knew well the dangers of such water. On coming aboard they all washed down with almost neat Dettol (disinfectant) to reduce the chance of Black Water Fever, and Alhagi was horrified to find a three-inch long leech sucking blood from his penis. He was most put out, and after treating it with salt he wanted the first aid box and used the whole tube of antiseptic. He kept telling us how he was newly married and he wanted to see a doctor at the next town. They all insisted on tight fitting swimming trunks before they went in the river again. These we bought in WARRI the next day.

Getting anchors up was another problem. We heaved and strained and struggled and Starboard came up with a dead tree sitting across the prongs. Four of us then went to work on Port and Gene edged forward until the chain was vertical. We then took a turn on the Sampson Post and went onto full hover. After taking in the slack and lifting four times, a very big dead tree came into sight. Using mooring ropes onto the cleats we were able to drop the anchor clear, bring it inboard, and then dropped the tree back into the depths.

Progress from there on was steady and after another hour the creeks seemed to widen and became straighter for longer periods. The vegetation changed and here were mostly Mangrove swamps. These trees stand tall and fairly straight, with a light grey, almost white bark, but their real characteristic is their roots. About 10ft above the mud the single trunk splits into hundreds of roots which spread in all directions so that the tree appears to be standing on a pedestal of woven legs.

At 16:40 we crossed the estuary of the Benin River. This was oil producing country and there were many tracks cut through the trees where pipelines passed and at night the sky was lit up in many directions by the waste gas burning off from the oil wells.

Our way led us out into the estuary of the Escarvos River. It was good to smell the salt air again but we soon turned inland once more to cross country and arrive at the Warri River.

It was here that we opened up the engines to 1950 RPM and starboard started humping 200 RPM. A quick shutdown showed the primary fuel filter to be full of water. This we cleared and then proceeded unhindered, and as light faded we came alongside a mud bank with a two hut settlement known as Inorin Fishing Camp.

The deafening silence after shutdown was fantastic. We shook hands with the local inhabitants, apparently all one family, and whilst a son was asking for some dash, the father was offering one of his daughters (about ten years old), for what purpose we didn't bother to find out.

We rigged mosquito nets over the aft doors and laid out beds, and after a brief supper of cold ham sandwiches and coffee, everyone was ready for bed.

The night was deep and dreamless apart from the occasional Kamikaze mosquito attacks. After nine hours and fifty-five minutes of Hovercraft travel I was past caring.

Monday 25th July 1977. Gene was up in the middle of the night, or at least that's how it seemed, in actual fact it was a little after 05:00. I rose in a zombie like condition, pulled on my coveralls and automatically started doing the DI (Daily Inspection) to a chorus from a million bullfrogs and the curious stares of the thousands of crabs sitting on the mud bank.

A quick mug of coffee and at 06:40 our roaring engines were shattering the dawn. It was a beautiful time of day, as indeed early mornings are anywhere. At 08:00 we were tying up at the IWD (Inland Waterways Department) wharf in Warri. It was a stout wooden pier with a fuel pump and water tap where we all took make-shift baths.

Once spruced up and uniformed, Capt. Akiou and I went in search of the local D Mar O (District Marine Officer). This was in fact the headquarters of the IWD. We were to organize refueling, whilst Gene and the AB's stayed onboard proudly showing hundreds of curious interested parties over the craft.

After much hand-shaking and introductions, fuel was arranged. By using the large bore hose from the hand bilge pump and with three men to hold it up high, we were able to fill all of our drums in position, taking onboard 1002 liters.

Fresh water drums were re-filled, and all this time more and ıore onlookers were filing through the boat.

All was ready and by 11.25 we took on the local D Mar O and goodness knows how many others for a ten minute demonstration up river and back again. On our return there was again much handshaking (In the Rivers State even handshaking is significant and it must be done in a certain style which I soon picked up).

The Craft was ours again and the wide open waterway our horizon. It was almost as if we begrudged the mass intrusion of what, after all, had become our home. Everyone's spirits rose as we passed clear of civilization. Even the craft seemed sprightlier.

The day was overcast with frequent heavy deluges of rain, but the way was mostly wide, although an additional problem arose with vast areas of floating water lilies'. We reduced the lift to 2000 RPM in an attempt to push the plants out of the way, but even so, raw water filters on average were choked four times per hour, sometimes more.

About 13:30 at a place called Esanma we stopped for the crew to pick up food. The only way to land here was to put the bow up on the mud bank and hold the craft against the current using two engines, one against the other.

The rain was torrential and everyone was slipping and sliding around in the mud. As we backed off we nearly tipped a native out of his canoe, and then proceeded to wind his fishing net into the port propeller. It was painful to stand on the aft deck, the water pouring off me as I watched a long line of fishing floats fall into file behind us. However, something snapped and suddenly the floats were no longer following but bobbing around in abandoned confusion. We were free and seemingly undamaged.

The afternoon and the rain continued as we entered Akiou's childhood territory. We reached the village of seaman Nama and once again we put our bows on the bank so that he could pay a brief visit to his family. Next was a village of a recently retired D Mar O and Akiou went ashore again, slipping and sliding on the muddy embankment to exchange greetings for some ten to fifteen minutes.

The journey continued and words were exchanged between Sampou and Akiou because a detour could not be made to pass Sampou's village.

Not surprisingly, we arrived at Amasoma, the home town of Capt. Akiou about 17:00. There was much horn blowing and boat moving as we came alongside a fairly new floating pontoon. The whole town turned out to see us; thousands of wide eyed children catching every word. This was Akiou's day. He was a big man in his very own town.

Gene and I, as we ate our Irish stew on the aft deck that night, felt very much in sympathy with the animals in the zoo. I even felt pangs of guilt about eating in front of so many hungry children. Nothing was wasted; even our used paper cups became cherished possessions of the children.

Later that evening Gene and I took a stroll and saw our first views of wildlife in the form of a lizard some four feet long being carried by one of the locals.

Despite our passing through two game parks and areas renowned for crocodile, hippos, boas and many other of God's creatures we were yet to observe any such species.

In the center of Amasoma was a flagpole and the tomb of a great past chief who, if the dates are to be believed, was 130 years old when he died.

Just then an emissary of Captain Akiou's household approached us and invited us to follow. We were led through a maze of mud and clay houses to one house in particular that was surrounded by a throng of people all jostling to see through the windows. We were led into a small room crammed with old men whose gnarled faces were highlighted by the three or four paraffin lamps that were burning. These were the chiefs and elders of the town, and they were bestowing upon us one of the highest honors that they could.

Beers were passed around and the chief (through an interpreter) made a long speech of welcome which was followed by many toasts and more speeches. It was obvious that everyone was well oiled, and when the native gin came around I decided to miss out. Gene took a tot and nearly blew his head off, much to the amusement of at least 200 children crammed at the windows.

After an hour or so Akiou came to our rescue and after a final toast, to which everyone chorused "God Bless" before downing the fire water, we took our leave.

The night was mild and damp. A thousand fireflies danced to the cricket's song and I was reluctant to go to sleep, but once my head touched mattress all else was oblivion.

Tuesday 26th July. Gene was up in the middle of the night again, somewhere about 05:30 and shortly after the craft slowly came awake. The skies were still grey and as I pottered around the DI with Sampou, a light drizzle was falling.

After breakfast we sat around waiting for Akiou to return and at 07:00 the honorable Captain, with a vast entourage of children, came striding along the mud bank.

Amid cheering and horn blowing, we slipped away from the berth heading down river to collect Mr. Subou, who had the evening before taken a canoe ride down to his village to visit his sick mother.

Subou safely onboard at 07:33 we proceeded south, mile after mile. First rain then sun and then more rain. After another half hour Subou took over from Akiou and for the first time behind the wheel of a Hovercraft, showed surprising ability. Mr. Subou from here on was to do much of the piloting with Gene keeping watch over the controls.

The scenery here was slowly changing. Large areas of grassland could be seen and the jungle areas were sparser. The townships we passed were well built, many of them with steel pontoon landing stages.

Akiou and Subou would frequently point out places and

things of interest as we passed, but the facts we received were far too many to remember.

By 09.55 we were almost on the coast again, crossing the Nun estuary at Akassa and then back into the mangrove swamps, moving east to the Brass River at 10.35, doubling back and going inland once more.

There was to be no breaks for food this time, as we were intending reaching Port Harcourt by nightfall.

Between the Nicholes River and the San Bartholomeo River our course changed, doubled back and retraced so many times that it could not even be followed on the map.

Imagine thousands of square miles of mangrove swamps, no signposts or villages; even a compass course is of no use because those creeks leading in the right direction often ended up going in the wrong direction.

Captain Akiou once told me the secret of his ability to navigate such an area. It is not done by secret signs or an inbuilt instinct, but simply by counting. The third creek on the left, then the fifth right and so on and so on. How he found the deep water channels was to follow the line of drifting Water Lilies as moving water cut the deepest channel. In all fairness to the Captain, we only touched bottom once in all that way, which must give credit to his techniques.

At 14:40 we reached Abonema on the Sambrelro River, and this appeared to be quite a big town for this area, with a church and some quite nice brick built houses.

From there on, the way opened up into the Buguma Creek, which led us by 15:15 into the deep sea lane of the New Calabar River, arriving at Port Harcourt at 16:00. Along this last section the craft fair flew along, sensing that only a short ninety-mile sea trip was left between us and journeys end.

Wednesday 27th July 1977. Although Gene and I had been keen take a shore run here, our unshaven state and the fact that

Captain Abakoba, a senior marine officer with the IWD, was expected, deterred us from leaving the craft the previous evening.

Now, after rising not too early, Gene decided that we could make Calabar on the fuel that we had left, and so, after taking on fresh water, we awaited the return of Captain Akiou who had been dispatched to locate Abakoba.

We tested the air con and found all OK and then got busy putting double lashings on everything moveable.

At 11:15 Akiou returned without Abakoba and we were underway by 11:40. It took an hour to reach the sea and then we found out! As soon as we poked our bow out we were in very troubled waters. The line of buoys led out for ten miles and we had to reach the last one (The Fairway Buoy) before turning up the coast. The skies were dark and threatening, and the sea was everywhere.

With a combination of millions of gallons of water coming down the rivers, a rising tide and two sand bars, this was no place for a hovercraft.

The seas were only eight to twelve feet but they were two per craft length. We banged shook and shuddered, at times shipping whole waves over the bow while Gene expertly juggled the throttles and the River men sat rigid. After nearly an hour of bone jarring, we had only reached buoy 1L, about seven miles. Gene and I decided to turn back.

The return run was fantastic as we surfed along the crest of each wave, and in twenty minutes we were back in smooth waters. We turned to starboard and crept into a tiny place called Bonny. Gene trudged off through the rain to search out some charts for the sea channel (for which we had none), and also to purchase some more fuel.

At 14:00 Gene returned looking dejected. There was no fuel or charts or pilots in Bonny, so we set off back up river to Port Harcourt, stopping on the way to allow Gene to board a Greek ship and to take a look at their charts. We then, at least, had the navigational information to reach Calabar.

In Port Harcourt we tried for fuel at the BP fueling jetty, but it was after four and besides I.W.D. owed them money, so we proceeded to the police post where we were allowed to tie up for the night.

Good old Akiou was dispatched with 80 Naira and two empty oil drums in a taxi to purchase some fuel from the nearest filling station.

Just alongside the Police Station was a bloated corpse lying face up in the water. The city coroners had been called, but in order to prevent the poor unfortunate from drifting away, the police had attached a rope to its leg and passed it around a tree on the bank. The body was still there next morning.

Thursday 28th July 1977. It was morning again. My systems were revitalized by that first mug of hot sweet coffee.

Engines started and at 07:00 we were off to do battle with the sea again. I stood on the aft deck all the way down river, blowing the last vestiges of sleep from my head.

Forty five minutes later we were meeting the sea again. We ploughed on, passing an oil rig supply ship on her way in, but by 08:15 it was obvious we were getting nowhere quickly. We turned around and came shooting and sliding on the wave tops back to the security of the inlet and then proceeded on up to Port Harcourt IWD Jetty.

The local D Mar O was surprised to see us back so soon and he informed us that Abakoba had been there, but was now on the way to the airport to fly to Calabar. So leaving Sampou to organize some more fuel, Gene, Akiou and I went with the D Mar O to the airport.

Abakoba was there all right, and I took an instant dislike to him as he suggested we rush back to the craft and head out again for Calabar. Gene and I however persuaded Abakoba to wait until the next morning. We had a hot shower and a clean Hotel bed on our thoughts.

Abakoba took us to the Olympia Hotel and Gene and I took

one room for seventy Naira. The hot shower was a dream that didn't materialize but we settled for a clean bath.

I returned to the craft to collect my gear and found Sampou had gone ashore. Fuel was being delivered by IWD at our expense, at the police jetty, so Akiou and I moved the boat to the Police Jetty which was eight miles downriver from the IWD. The remainder of the afternoon I waited for the fuel to arrive, thinking all the time of that hotel food and clean bed.

Finally four drums of fuel arrived at the same time as Mr. Sampou and together we transferred with bilge pump from the quay to our inboard drums. By the time I arrived back at the Olympic, Gene was awake and ready to eat, so I cleaned up rapidly and went down stairs. On the desk was a notice saying there were no meals available but transport was provided to take any guests to the Presidential Hotel for dinner. We asked about transport but of course there wasn't any, so we took a five Naira cab ride.

The Presidential was as the name suggests quite grand and we had chicken and chips followed by a treat in the cinema to a very old Rock Hudson, swashbuckling adventure.

When we returned to the Olympic, we had a night cap in the bar with Abakoba. Our plans of a 05:30 start were not acceptable to him as he wanted to take breakfast first.

Friday 29th July. Hotel breakfast over, we got onboard about 07:40, Captain Abakoba taking up the navigator's seat with his books and charts as Gene and I exchanged knowing winks.

There was an additional crew member onboard that morning, a Mr. Thompson Ogbotoga, who was to be our Calabar pilot and first trainee in that region.

We passed Bonny at 08:20 and hit the sea (literally), a few minutes later. Whilst everyone braced for the first pounding, Abakoba's pencils and books went shooting in all directions. As green wave after green wave curtained the windscreen, I adjusted Abakoba's seatbelt to suit his generous waistline.

It was one hour and seven miles before he agreed to turn back. Once again we surfed and slid into Bonny, but this time Thompson took over the navigator's seat and led us on through the creeks towards Opobo.

It was low tide and we passed through some precariously narrow channels, sometimes with sandbanks only a few feet away. At such times we would slow to 1600 RPM and put 2800 RPM on the lift to gently tiptoe over the danger spots.

12:00 and we tied up to a concrete quay, where there was such a strong current running that we decided to keep all engines going for safety.

Abakoba, Akiou and Thompson went ashore to try and obtain the services of a local pilot that could take us from Opobo to rejoin the sea. An hour later they returned in the company of a wizened old man with a stubbly chin and sparse moustache who walked with surprising nimbleness for his apparent age.

I learnt later that much bargaining and drinking had to be done before he decided to join us, and even then he was reluctant.

Underway once more the jungle here was very dense and lightly populated. After only thirty minutes we were met by the breathtaking sight of the sea again, but everywhere, ahead, port and starboard seemed to be boiling surf and breakers.

We did a swift hard-a-port and came right along parallel to the beach and only a 100 yards or less from it. This was the tropical paradise type of area, with tall palms, thatched huts, and miles of silver sand. I could not have wished to go aground in a nicer place.

Slowly we gained sea room, working away from the shoreline at a shallow angle of no more than five degrees. The waves were broadside on and we sped effortlessly along their valleys, rolling but thankfully no longer pitching as we went.

There was a good deal of spray around, and occasionally Gene had to kill the lift to save ourselves from blowing over too far. I was concerned that I may have to refuel under these conditions, we were on half tanks then, but by my calculations we should have enough.

The afternoon passed on and we were skipping and flying along, at what seemed a terrific pace. Just after 16:00 we made the Calabar channel buoy and everyone let out a cheer and broke out a bottle of Schnapps. The little wizened pilot seemed to come alive and downed his Schnapps like it was going out of fashion.

Another hour up river and Calabar Town came in sight. We tied alongside and old landing craft, painted entirely in silver, at the IWD wharf.

There was old "Snowflake" and Eddie Twiggs and the kids all waiting. Eddie told us that everyone had been looking out for the flashing Hover light for the last couple of days.

We were descended upon by 100 IWD personnel all ready to clean and spruce but by popular request from our crew, we just locked up the doors, handed over the keys and headed for our hotel.

- The estimated total distance from Lagos to Calabar was 600 nautical miles.
- The fuel consumed totaled 4193 liters (1107.7 US Gallons)
- The total number of hours underway was thirty-nine.

We soon settled down in Calabar at the Hotel Metropole despite there being an ongoing strike of the hotel workers, with no meals, or room cleaning service etc. By July 31st we had had enough and following a showdown with Herbert Snowball, we finally moved into a government guest house.

The first few days we did many demonstration runs and press runs and even ran a special trip for the Military Governor, Major Omu. On this trip we actually had ninety-eight people onboard.

One evening we met Mr. John Page in a local restaurant. He was from England but had lived for many years in this region of Nigeria. He spoke perfect Pigeon English to communicate with the locals. He invited us to visit his Sawmill and Plywood factory and to have dinner in the PALMOL Club.

The next evening we were picked up and driven out through dense jungle and rubber plantations, stretching off into the gloom. At a sharp bend in the road we were startled to see a clearing, and laid out before us was an immaculate, cultivated and pristinely mown cricket field, complete with large white site screens, and a score tally board. Beyond the cricket field was a majestic club house, with dining terrace and a verandah that ran around the building. We were given a tour and admired all the trophies and cups on display. It was like stepping back into the last century.

We were treated like Royalty, and given a sumptuous meal. We retired for coffee and liqueurs to John Page's home, before returning to Calabar.

Once the craft was put into full service we were able to establish a routine. We trained the mechanics as quickly as possible. Re-fueling was still time consuming as fuel was brought to the jetty in drums and had to be pumped aboard. Most runs were completely full.

Our biggest challenge was to keep the air conditioning going. The demand was high, and both units could not keep up. The ambient temperature was around 90 degrees F with a humidity of around 85%. The doors would be opened for passenger loading, the passenger's bodies and clothing were very warm, and it was expected that the air conditioning could create a 20–30 degree drop in temperature on a thirty minute run.

We were working on average twelve hour days at this time.

Gene Proch was relieved by John Barber who arrived in Calabar on August 13th. Gene flew out on the 14th and I moved back to the Metropolitan hotel on the 17th.

The 5th of September was memorable for the fact that I dived the Calabar River in order to assist placing the craft onto a slip-

Peter White being greeted by the Head of Rivers State during an inauguration ceremony. Libation was offered to the River Goddess for safe journeys

ping trolley at a dilapidated shipyard once owned by a British Company in the 1930s. The craft had suffered severe impact damage due to operating after dark. Captain John Barber had been asked to delay his departure in order to wait for the State Governor, who was returning to Calabar. As a consequence he hit some debris in the dark and severely damaged the craft propellers.

We did a lot of research around the Calabar area, checking out cranes and repair yards, but in the end the slipway at the Sescot yard seemed the only viable option. We were able to participate in preparing the slipping trolley and support blocks; fortunately, as the yard manager could not conceive the layout of a catamaran hull.

Leaving the completion of the repairs to my trainees, the next morning I set out on yet another adventure. I was to return to Lagos by road with one of the IWD drivers.

We drove to Aba, Oworri, and Onitsha. By 18:00 we were crossing the Niger Bridge, then on to Olu and finally arrived in Benin City. The road was very rough and sections had such large mud and water filled potholes that one was in danger of losing your complete vehicle in the hole. Everyone was twisting and swerving, trying to pick a way through what was reminiscent of a battle field on the Somme during the First World War.

We saw two bad accidents. One was an overturned bus, with passengers injured and strewn all about. No one was stopping to help as the fear of hijackers, robbers, and murderers was very real. They are attracted to accidents like vultures to a dying animal.

As night was falling, the traffic began to drive at breakneck speed in order to reach the safety of the city before dark. Even the police did not venture far from the city after dusk.

The next morning we were on the road by 06:30. The road was still rough with many dangerously narrow bridges. We finally made it into Lagos by 15:00 where my first task was to go to the stores to locate a replacement propeller for Calabar and to get it shipped ASAP.

The next few days were spent, organizing parts and reporting on the Calabar operation to the Cross River State Office, Secretary to the Permanent Secretary. Our only communication with Calabar was through this office, via Shortwave Radio. Our conversations were relayed via radio operators, and their translation of our instructions which were often hilarious and frequently misunderstood.

I flew out on the 16th on a Sabena flight to Brussels and on to London. After a brief vacation (I had been invited to visit Gene Proch in Florida) I was back at Hovermarine ready for the next challenge.

FLORIDA TO BOSTON

October 18, 1978 found me flying out of London's Heathrow Airport once again, this time bound for Orlando, Florida, via New York and Tampa.

The job was to run trials and testing on a US built, re-furbished HM216, and then drive it up to Boston for a charter with the Commonwealth of Massachusetts, a mere 1,250 nautical mile run.

I arrived in Orlando in the middle of a warm, humid night and was met by my old friend, Captain John Barber. We drove over to Titusville, whilst catching up on each other's news, and checked into the Quality Inn for a good night's rest.

Early next morning I was up and raring to go. We had a great American breakfast in Sambo's restaurant for ninety-nine cents, including endless coffee. Ninety nine cents, can you believe it! I was starting to love America.

Our plan for the trip was to travel the Intracoastal Waterway as far as Norfolk, Virginia, and then a quick dash up the New Jersey shore, then into Long Island Sound and on up to Cape Cod. Gene Proch, (Captain and colleague on the Lagos to Calabar trip) was also coming along to do some of the driving and navigating.

Saturday 21st October 1978. We were underway by 08:30, skimming across the calm waters, as free as any bird, eating up the miles as we rushed northwards. As the craft settled down we grew accustomed to the noise and the harmonic vibrations of a well-tuned machine.

After running for eighty-three miles we came alongside at Marine World at 12:15, where I was able to rectify a few water leaks. By 13:00 we were on our way again, all the way to Jacksonville where we arrived at 15:15, another sixty miles nearer to our destination.

We took on fuel (198 gallons), and prepared for inspection by the Florida branch of the United States Coastguard.

Monday 23rd October. After an eventful morning, John Barber and Gene Proch had a disagreement, as a result of which Gene returned home and John and I were left to carry on alone. The Coast Guard inspection went well, and by 13:15 we were once more northbound. The craft flew along, and I felt very happy and privileged to be onboard.

Navigation of the Intracoastal water way was relatively straight forward. The channels were well marked with Red or Green posts, numbered and lit. It was easy to look up the number of the channel marker post and to find it on the chart in order to get an exact fix on our position.

In some areas (Manatee habitats for example) there were strictly enforced speed limits which we were obliged to observe.

We were soon leaving Florida and entering Georgia, and at a point near the Okefinokee Swamp we ran foul of some heavy vegetation that virtually stalled the starboard engine. We deployed anchors, and, as I was the only spare hand onboard, I went over the side, knife in hand, to cut the vegetation free from the propeller, whilst John stood sentry-like, armed with the boathook, to defend me against any curious alligators that might come around. Needless to say, I was very quick!

Back on board, we soon recovered anchors and getting back on track moving from the Amelia River to the East River in South Georgia. We crossed Blackbeard Creek and the Ogeechee River, finally arriving in Savannah by 19:15, where we took on 207 gallons of fuel and then headed for a very welcome bed at the Thunderbird Motel. Our average speed for the day was 29.13 miles per hour.

The next day we continued through the Intracoastal Waterway, taking turns at the helm, thus allowing each other to take breaks and to get food.

Driving along the Intracoastal was comparable to freeway driving, and the miles flew by with few of the challenges that we had met in Nigeria. At least at this time we were able to enjoy the passing scenery and admire some of the spectacular waterside properties. Around 15:30 p.m. we stopped for fuel at Belle Island, NC, near Charleston. We then continued for another hour and a quarter to arrive in Myrtle Beach at 17:15.

Wednesday 25th October. This morning in Myrtle Beach we took advantage of a local Scuba Diver, and for a few bucks he was willing to replace the missing attachment shackles on the forward skirt segments. By 08:45 we were underway up the Intracoastal. Everything was running well as we crossed the "Cape Fear River" over into North Carolina.

Around 13:30 we pulled into Swansboro, NC, and refueled. With 156 miles already under the cushion today, we were making excellent progress.

By 13:45 we were heading north and east again as the route dictated. Crossing Pamlico Sound, the route was more exposed to the Atlantic wind, the Sound only being separated from the ocean by a chain of small islands. We turned inland here and came to rest in Belhaven for the night and to take on more fuel.

*Thursday 26th Octobe*r. Underway from Belhaven by 8:15, we headed up the Pungo River and into a perfectly straight canal that brought us across to the Alligator River.

A journey such as this could not have been possible if it wasn't for the outstanding work and foresight of the Army Corps of Engineers. The systems of waterways and bridges so excellently built and maintained are an inspiration to the World.

Crossing the Albemarle Sound we returned to the coast for a

short while, before heading inland again on the North Landing River and the Elizabeth River to arrive at Chesapeake City, Virginia. A few more miles on the Elizabeth and we arrived in Portsmouth, Virginia at 14:15.

Friday 27th October. This day started off a bit differently. We started out on the continuing trip north, but after thirty minutes it became obvious that the temporary repair to the sea water filter would not be sustainable. We went to a berth in Norfolk and from there by taxi to a machine shop in downtown Norfolk. A new filter cap was fabricated from aluminum, and we were able to pick it up before the end of the morning. Once everything was back together and the oil leak had been cleaned up, we set off again around 14:30.

As we entered Chesapeake Bay, we heard a Coastguard warning over the VHF radio advising that a small cargo ship had lost part of her deck cargo overboard. She had been carrying sawn logs!

We became extremely vigilant as contact with any one of these logs at speed could have been disastrous for the HM2. Slowly the shadows lengthened as the sun began to set, and to us it seemed that every second wave had a log hidden in the shadow of the trough. We were thankful to come alongside a marina on the Yeocomico River, right on the Virginia, Maryland border, having avoided damage so far.

Saturday 28th October. Determined to make up for lost time, we agreed on an early start this morning. By 06:45 we were underway and rounding Point Lookout, before turning north again, heading for Annapolis, where we came alongside for fuel at 10:35.

From Annapolis we headed north again, passing Baltimore en-route for Chesapeake City, Maryland.

It was in this area that we were surprised to see another flashing yellow light, proceeding some two miles ahead of us. Could this be another hovercraft of which we knew nothing about? We were under a speed restriction in this section, and so we were not closing on the mysterious yellow light.

Upon consulting the navigation guide it became clear that the vessel was a nuclear submarine, the only vessel other than a hovercraft that is required to display a flashing yellow light whilst underway. The submarine flash rate was however slower than that of a hovercraft.

Once past Baltimore, we resumed full cruising speed until we turned into Back Creek and the approach to Chesapeake City, Delaware.

You cannot imagine the thrill it was for me to see all these famous sites from the water. It was one of the most memorable trips of my life.

From Chesapeake City we continued east through the canal to emerge into the Delaware River. Turning south for the first time since leaving Florida, we hurtled down to the Cape May canal, and thankfully tied up for the night in Cape May harbor.

Sunday 29th October. After an early breakfast we were at sea by 07:15. What a difference between the Intracoastal Waterway and the open Atlantic Ocean. We knew we were in for a tough ride from the start, with waves and wind against our progress.

The HM2 hovercraft was a very lively vessel when out in the open ocean. Because of her relatively light weight, and the potential for a good speed, the hull was influenced directly by any waves greater than our skirt depth. The catamaran hull was very safe but as the vessel rolled the buoyancy of the submerging hull increased exponentially, creating a rapid righting moment. Combine this with the pitching that was dampened by the inflated AB loop as we impacted the troughs of the waves, but power had to be drawn back as we plunged and re-applied to climb up the next wave.

We reached the North Little Egg River before concluding that we would not reach Sandy Hook with the current fuel left onboard. We made a rolling turn and headed back for Atlantic City, and were alongside at 13:00

Monday 30th October. The weather was still rough, and so we were able to carry out running repairs onboard, clean the vessel up a little, as well as catch up with washing our clothes etc.

Tuesday 31st October. Finally the winds had eased and taking advantage of the early morning calm we emerged out into the Atlantic Ocean at 06:45. The sea state was reasonable as we dashed forever northwards. For the next ninety miles we zipped past the New Jersey coastline until we were able to turn inland at Sandy Hook.

With the spectacular New York City skyline looming before us, within five more miles we were passing under the Verrazzano Bridge. The Statute of Liberty and Ellis Island slipped past on the port side as we hung a right into the East River. Under the Brooklyn and Manhattan Bridges, we continued up the East River past Queens until finally we were under the Throgs Neck Bridge and out into Long Island Sound. Absolutely awesome!

Having done the whole New York hover past, it was good to open throttles and get back up to our cruising speed. Another fifty miles and we were coming alongside in Newhaven Connecticut at 13:45. After a late lunch, we were again able to carry out some running maintenance, (an exhaust bracket on the main engine had failed), plus cleaning up and preparing the engines for what tomorrow would bring.

Wednesday 1st November. By 08:50 we had slipped the moorings and were underway once more, leaving New Haven Harbor and heading East North East up Long Island Sound. Thirty five miles on this heading and we were parallel to Montauk Point. Passing out of the shelter of Long Island we were once again exposed to the rigors of the North Atlantic. The sea was getting very rough and the craft was getting a hard workout.

Forty miles farther and we were entering Buzzards Bay. The wind had shifted more to the north and so the further up the bay we progressed the more shelter we were getting from the land mass of Cape Cod.

Another twenty miles and we were entering the Cape Cod Canal. Passing thru the four mile canal we were hopeful of making Boston by nightfall.

As we emerged from the canal all hell broke loose. There were ten-foot waves in all directions, as the craft hammered and banged us around in complete abandon. At that precise moment the lift engine died, with the re-start circuits and all power to the lift engine lost.

Leaving John to wrestle with the craft I dived below to investigate the failure. For some reason, put it down to experience or instinct, I was able to pin-point the problem straight away. Apparently the forward batteries had not been secured in their location, and in the rough slamming we had just received, the batteries had become disconnected.

I advised John of what had happened, and told him to re-start the lift engine as soon as I re-made the connection, which I would indicate by banging on the wheelhouse floor, the batteries being in stowage below the wheelhouse.

I re-made the connection, and signaled the re-start. John now had a better control of the craft, but I had to remain in the stowage wedged between the deck head and the batteries, in order to prevent the connections from parting again.

We made a perilous turnaround, and with just a glimpse of the markers, leading back to the canal being visible from the peaks of each wave, John skillfully brought us back into the shelter of the canal. We motored the four miles back to a marina at Onset near the beginning of the canal.

Once tied alongside, we set about tidying the craft, re-lashing loosened equipment, and I secured the forward batteries. We found out that the Marina was closed up for the winter. (It was after all November in the North Atlantic, with not much pleasure sailing going on). There was also no fuel available.

It was after dark by the time we had finished our tasks and when we came to the marina gates we found we were locked in. We had to scale a fence to get out, and then scout around for a taxi to take us to a motel that was open.

Thursday 2nd November. We were able to walk to the Marina and climbed back over the fence, and by 07:30 we were all ready to depart. We were both very concerned as to whether there was enough fuel to get us to Boston fifty five miles away. Once underway we were continually monitoring the fuel gauges, and re-calculating distance to run against current consumption. It looked as though we wouldn't make it on the fuel that we had left.

Fortunately, anchored out in Massachusetts Bay, was a large ocean going tug, preparing to haul an oil rig from Boston to the Indian Ocean. We went alongside and the Dutch crew turned out to be very friendly and helpful. They passed us down a hose and gave us ten gallons of fuel, refusing all offers of payment.

With this small margin, we proceeded with confidence into Boston Harbor, Coming alongside Rowes Wharf at 10:45. We were well received by all at Massachusetts Bay Lines and treated to a nice lunch in the famous Park Plaza Hotel on Boston Common.

John sent a memorable telex announcing our arrival, with the words that read, "A loose collection of varied parts, flying in tight formation, has landed in Boston."

- The estimated total distance from Titusville to Boston was 1,486 nautical Miles.
- The fuel consumed totaled 1,949 US Gallons
- The total hours underway were 67.75 hours.
- The average speed for the entire trip was 22 knots.

OSLO, NORWAY

In April 1989 I was asked if I would help prepare our old friend, Craft 485 (now ex-Harbor Bay), for a charter in Oslo, Norway. Thankfully the craft was still in good condition, perhaps in part as a result of the TLC that we were able to lavish on it during our San Francisco stay.

A Kenny Rogers CD was the only music that I brought along for the trip. We played it at full volume for hours at a time and we soon had the three mad Vikings all singing along in unison.

Our Norseman captain was Staale Ostbye, and his two compadres were both of similar stature, and I felt in good hands and in a stout vessel, well prepared for the dash across the North Sea.

We set off for an easy run to Dover on May 31st (a Wednesday). The craft flew along and everyone was in good spirits. The first 130 miles were completed in good time'

Day two we took off out of Dover headed straight across the English Channel in observance of the critically enforced traffic separation system and headed up the French and Belgian coastline. Our destination was Scheveningen in Holland. We rode the 115 miles quite comfortably and were alongside in time for a good dinner. Kenny Rogers was with us all the way. Nobody suggested buying any different music, so KR was to be the theme for the whole trip.

On June 2nd, we set off out of Scheveningen in a very light early morning mist. The Dutch coast was hard to navigate around as the land was so low-lying, but the Dutch did a great job with their buoyage and channel markers. The morning turned into a perfect day, with bright sun and light breezes. We arrived in Den Halder, which was only fifty-five miles.

Saturday, June 3rd, we left Den Halder after re-fueling on a much more interesting section of the journey. We cut inside of the Frisian Islands and proceeded northeast to Cuxhaven before turning inland on the river Elbe. After 165 miles of smooth running we turned into the Kiel Canal at Brunsbuttel.

The Kiel Canal was an engineering marvel that over the years must have saved millions of gallons of fuel for vessels bound for the heart of Germany or the Baltic Sea. There were speed restrictions on the canal, and so we were able to enjoy the scenery and admire the spectacular bridges over the next thirty-eight miles. We tied up in Kiel and spent a good night with a few beers and a great dinner after covering the largest distance of the trip so far.

Day five of our trip, we set out from Kiel, heading north up the Skagerrak, the body of water that separates Sweden from Denmark. The navigation was wide and we were able to cruise at a decent 30 knots all the way to Grena'a in northeast Denmark. We had covered another 150 miles towards journey's end.

Grena'a was a very rural port dedicated almost entirely to the fishing industry. Once we had refueled craft and bodies, we cranked up Kenny Rogers and headed out into the open and exposed Swedish coast. After sixty-five miles we cleared Skagen, the most northerly tip of Denmark. We could see storm clouds gathering behind us. We still had 110 miles to reach our destination of Horten, about halfway down the Oslo Fjord.

With throttles full open, we raced the storm. The craft flew along, like a thoroughbred, and as Horten came into sight, the rain caught up. We came alongside amid wind and heavy rain, but we were safe.

Total distance run: Approx 828 miles in six days.

I stayed on a few days and helped set up the service between the airport, downtown Oslo, and the most popular beaches.

I was back again in 1991 to survey the craft in preparation for yet another charter.

Now, looking back, I must surely hold the record for the most miles covered on an HM2. Just three trips, up the west coast of Nigeria, the east coast of the United States, and Southampton – Oslo, totaled nearly 3,000 miles. Add in countless cross-Channel delivery trips and regular operations and I must have logged over 4,000 miles. I loved every minute of it!

ACKNOWLEDGMENTS

WE OWE AN ENORMOUS DEBT of gratitude to Alan Blunden, Publisher and Editor of *Fast Ferry International*. He provided most of the detail needed to construct the history of build and sales (Appendix C). His inputs on competition and many of the Hovermarine operations around the world filled in the many blanks in our memories. His extensive library of photographs provided visual testimony we would otherwise have not been able to incorporate into this story. Finally, from the start, his enthusiasm and effort for this project convinced us that if we wrote it, there might actually be an audience. Alan, many thanks.

More broadly, we acknowledge all the many people who worked so hard with us in those days to make the Hovermarine story.

Some are mentioned herein by name, but all are part of our memories.

A special thanks to those customers who were so vital to whatever success we managed, and who are no longer with us to revisit the memories. First among them is Edmond Lau. Also we remember Tacoma's City Manager Erling Mork and Fire Chief Tony Mitchell. They may be gone, but their legacy lives on as *Commencement*, still state-of-the-art in fireboats forty years later.

Finally, we acknowledge our publishers, Hellgate Press, whose efforts made this book all we ever hoped it would be.

www.hellgatepress.com